United States
Department
of Agriculture

Forest Service

General Technical
Report NC-266

April 2006

Forestry Cooperatives: What Today's Resource Professionals Need To Know

A satellite conference held November 18, 2003, St. Paul, MN.

Pamela Jakes, compiler

U.S. Department of Agriculture, Forest Service
North Central Research Station
1992 Folwell Avenue
St. Paul, MN 55108

www.ncrs.fs.fed.us

Contents

Introduction

Charlie Blinn[1]

Nonindustrial private forest (NIPF) land represents approximately 48 percent of the forest land cover in the United States and has played an important role in meeting an increasing domestic wood demand (Smith *et al.* 2004). Conscientious stewardship of these forests is a perennial issue facing natural resource professionals due to the large number of owners and their diverse interests. Landowner assistance programs such as the American Tree Farm System, the Forest Stewardship Program, and woodland owner associations exist to stimulate forest management and reforestation on these ownerships through subsidies of money and materials.

Today, some entrepreneurial NIPF landowners are developing forest landowner cooperatives—an old idea that has re-emerged with the growing interest in forest certification and the allure of increased profit through the value-added processing of timber products. Forest landowner cooperatives are defined as "user-owned and user-controlled forestry-related businesses that distribute benefits to members on the basis of their use." They generally share two characteristics: (1) they are jointly owned and managed by members who are NIPF landowners, and (2) members equitably share the costs and benefits of maintaining/operating the cooperative. Today's forest landowner cooperatives, like those in the past, look to provide members with services otherwise unavailable, such as improved access to markets and increased revenue from forest management. Unlike prior efforts, these organizations also tend to foster sustainable forestry (e.g., forest certification), land protection, and ecological restoration.

In recent years, a number of regional nonprofit, government, and university organizations have begun to support and educate NIPF owners interested in forming cooperatives. However, many natural resource professionals have only cursory knowledge of the opportunities and barriers associated with cooperatives. Also, although cooperative development specialists are knowledgeable about cooperative formation, organizational structures, and management, they are generally not knowledgeable about forestry and NIPF landowners. Furthermore, natural resource professionals and cooperative development specialists know little about each other and the role they both can play in the development and support of forest landowner cooperatives.

The satellite conference "Forestry Cooperatives: What Today's Resource Professionals Need to Know" was broadcast on November 18, 2003. It was the brainchild of the Local

A cooperative, something that brings more sensitive management to the land, is certainly appealing because we want to protect what's here, we want to make it better, and we want to generate some income.

Blue Ridge Forest Cooperative Potential Member

There are many potential benefits from a cooperative. Marketing, access to markets, being able to label your products, getting landowners to communicate and voice their opinions effectively are probably the largest ones.

Lewis County, Washington, Potential Cooperative Member

[1] Department of Forest Resources, University of Minnesota, St. Paul, MN, cblinn@umn.edu

Forest Cooperatives Working Group—a joint venture of the University of Minnesota, the University of Wisconsin, and the USDA Forest Service. The conference was sponsored by the University of Minnesota College of Natural Resources, the University of Minnesota Extension Service, the University of Wisconsin Center for Cooperatives, the University of Wisconsin Extension Cooperative Extension, and the USDA Forest Service North Central Research Station. Funding was provided by the USDA Cooperative State Research, Education, and Extension Service (CSREES).

The satellite conference was designed to help natural resource professionals and cooperative development specialists to:

- Gain a better understanding of cooperatives and a deeper insight into some of the successes and challenges of cooperatives
- Evaluate whether the forestry cooperative model is right for a specific area and if so, how to further the discussion locally
- See how cooperatives can complement other landowner assistance programs such as Tree Farm, Forest Stewardship, and woodland owner associations
- Hear firsthand about the experiences of forestry cooperative initiatives from Massachusetts, Virginia, Michigan, Wisconsin, and Washington

This report summarizes much of the information presented during that satellite conference. It also includes a DVD of the case studies shown during the conference. We would like to thank the members of these cooperatives for sharing their stories with us and with our broader conference audience.

We would also like to thank Chery Hays Day, a Senior Media Resources Producer with the University of Minnesota Extension Service, for her outstanding videoconference production work and for her never-failing uplifting personality; John Day for playing the music lead-in to the video conference and for keeping everyone loose during the satellite uplink; and all of the staff at Minnesota Satellite and Technology (MnSAT) for facilitating the satellite conference uplink.

Literature Cited

Smith, W.B.; Miles, P.D.; Vissage, J.S.; Pugh, S.A. 2004. Forest resources of the United States, 2002. Gen. Tech. Rep. NC-241. St. Paul, MN: U.S. Department of Agriculture, Forest Service, North Central Research Station. 137 p.

Nonindustrial Private Forest Landowners and Sources of Assistance

Eli Sagor[1]

Nonindustrial private forest (NIPF) lands make up a large and important portion of the forested land base in the U.S. Forest management decisions on these lands have important impacts on the nature and level of benefits derived from the land. This chapter will review some important findings about NIPF owners as they relate to forest landowner cooperatives.

About NIPF Owners

Collectively, NIPF landowners are tremendously important to the condition of forested ecosystems and forest-dependent businesses. In 1994, NIPF lands in the United States totaled 232 million acres, or 59 percent of the total forest land (Birch 1996). NIPF lands account for a higher percentage of forest land in the Eastern United States than in the West.

NIPF landowners also accounted for 60 percent of all United States timber removals in 1997. This percentage is projected to rise between 1997 and 2050, particularly in the East (Haynes *et al.* 1995). The availability of timber from private forest lands is important to the long-term viability of domestic timber-producing companies and the people who work for them.

Figure 1.—*Parcelization is a potential threat to the long-term productivity of our forest land. (Photo credit: NCRS Image Library).*

[1] University of Minnesota Extension Service, St. Paul, MN, sagor001@umn.edu

NIPF parcels are becoming more numerous and smaller. This process, called parcelization, poses a potential threat to the long-term productivity of the forested land base. Between 1978 and 1994, the total amount of private woodlands increased by about 27 percent. However, during the same period, the total amount of this land in parcels of less than 100 acres increased by 73 percent, from 72 million to 124 million acres (Birch 1996). Most forest management activities are less economically feasible on smaller parcels than on larger parcels (Row 1978). Parcelization therefore has the potential to reduce forest land productivity (Kline *et al.* 2004). The potential diseconomy of scale of managing forests on so many small parcels has been a concern for the forestry community for many years (Alig *et al.* 1990, Skok and Gregersen 1975).

Despite the potential benefits of a high level of timber harvest from NIPF lands, management for timber is not a primary objective for many NIPF landowners. Numerous studies have found that most NIPF landowners consider financial returns from harvesting timber on their land to be of relatively minor importance (Alig *et al.* 1990, Bliss and Martin 1989, Elwood *et al.* 2003, Young and Reichenbach 1987). For many owners, nonmarket amenities and services such as wildlife habitat, recreation, and solitude are of greater interest.

Figure 2.—*For many nonindustrial private landowners, activities such as wildlife viewing are the primary reason for owning and managing their land. (Photo credit: R. Haack, NCRS).*

NIPF landowners consult a variety of information sources in making forestry decisions. Studies in Michigan (West *et al.* 1988) and Minnesota (Baughman *et al.* 1998) suggested that landowners prefer to obtain information from neighbors or peers rather than more distant sources. This preference may favor the development of landowner groups that foster dialogue among local landowners.

Existing Sources of Assistance

Most individual NIPF landowners have little knowledge or day-to-day access to information for making forest management decisions. Nor do they typically have an important financial incentive to find this information, because most do not consider financial returns to be a primary management concern. Nonetheless, numerous sources of information, technical assistance, education, and money are available to help NIPF landowners make and implement smart decisions for managing their forests. This section introduces and briefly discusses some of the most important sources of information and assistance available to most NIPF owners.

Technical assistance, cost sharing, education, and other programs provide NIPF landowners with information and assistance in the management of their woodlands. These initiatives and the research behind them have focused on the NIPF "problem" of relatively low timber harvest levels. By most assessments, these programs have been both efficient and effective (Cubbage *et al.* 1987, Esseks and Moulton 2000, Skok and Gregersen 1975).

Technical Assistance

Technical assistance programs offer NIPF landowners access to the services of professional foresters, soil conservation experts, or other natural resource professionals for reduced, or no, fees. Technical assistance also includes access to extension and other educational programs and resources. The most common services provided are direct, onsite forest management advice for landowners, education for landowners, and education for loggers, wood processors, and others (Cubbage *et al.* 1996, Egan *et al.* 2001). Assistance for landowners is designed to help them make informed decisions about what forest management activities to conduct and how to find resources necessary to implement them. Assistance for loggers is generally designed to promote the use of best forest management practices (BMPs) during timber harvest.

The availability of technical assistance programs has been shown to increase implementation of BMPs. In West Virginia, forest improvement practices recommended in a forest stewardship plan were more likely to be implemented than practices not recommended (Egan *et al.* 2001). Egan (1999) also found higher rates of implementation of BMPs on sales administered by a professional forester than on those in which a forester was not involved. Landowners also frequently mention the educational value of working one-on-one with a professional forester. Although independent, paid consultants are available in most situations, technical assistance programs often reach landowners who would not be willing to spend the necessary money to hire a private consultant. These programs, then, play a critical role in making landowners aware of the services that professional foresters provide.

Technical assistance programs have been found to be efficient and effective. The Forest Stewardship Program offers NIPF owners free or low-cost management plan development services provided by public or private professional foresters. Many states also make professional foresters available to advise landowners as they consider options for timber harvests or other forest practices. Cubbage *et al.* (1985) found a benefit of $600 per acre in net present value from working with a service forester in Georgia. The same study found that working with a forester also increased stumpage (standing timber) prices paid to NIPF owners by 58 percent. A subsequent study conducted in Minnesota found similar results: the average bid price on aspen sales was $4.66 per cord on sales assisted by a forester and only $3.32 on sales not assisted by a forester (Henly *et al.* 1988). Similar studies in other states have found similar results, if less pronounced than in the original study (Cubbage *et al.* 1996).

The benefits of forest landowner assistance programs have been shown to accrue not only to individual landowners, but also to society. Cubbage *et al.* (1985) found that government investments in the Georgia Rural Forestry Assistance program consistently provided positive returns at the individual and social levels.

Cost Share Programs

Cost share programs are funded and administered at the Federal, State, and local levels. Most of these programs are funded by the U.S. Department of Agriculture, and many originated from initiatives to maintain or restore water quality or the productivity of the agricultural and forested land base. In 1987, 14 States offered their own cost share programs (Bullard and Straka 1988). These programs included free tree seedlings, fencing, timber stand improvement, reforestation, and other activities.

Financial support for reforestation activities helps to ensure a sustained supply of wood products. Payments to support erosion control devices, wildlife habitat features, and similar items help maintain clean water and viable wildlife populations. Most studies of the value of technical assistance and cost share programs found them to be efficient and effective (Bullard and Straka 1988, Cubbage *et al.* 1985, Henly *et al.* 1988). These and similar studies generally found net positive returns for investments in private forestry assistance, but to varying degrees. However, others questioned the value of public funds used to influence what might otherwise be free markets.

Cost sharing increases the impact of technical assistance programs (Esseks and Moulton 2000). Royer (1987) found that reforestation behavior among southern NIPF owners was highly sensitive to price and the availability of cost share assistance. Where reforestation costs were high and cost share funds were not available, less reforestation occurred. State and provincial forestry agency directors considered technical assistance and cost share programs to be the most effective policy tools to influence behavior on NIPF lands (Kilgore and Blinn 2004).

In a survey of forest management program leaders, financial and technical assistance (referred to as educational programs, technical assistance, and fiscal incentives) were found to be the three policy options perceived to be most effective (Cheng and Ellefson 1993). Education and technical assistance in particular were perceived to be highly effective and efficient.

Education and Information

The Cooperative Extension Service, woodland owner associations, forest landowner cooperatives, and other organizations offer information and educational opportunities to NIPF owners. Organizations like the American Tree Farm System (ATFS), the National Woodland Owners' Association, and similar organizations at State and local levels are examples of woodland owner associations. As an example of the reach of these organizations, the ATFS currently has more than 65,000 members nationally, all of whom receive a monthly magazine with information landowners can use to better manage their woodlands.

Figure 3.—*Organizations such as Cooperative Extensions, woodland owner associations, and forest landowner cooperatives offer information and educational opportunities to nonindustrial private forest landowners. (Photo credit: E. Sagor).*

Regulatory Programs

Although they may exist for other reasons, forest practices regulatory systems can be important sources of information for landowners considering timber harvest. These systems can be voluntary or mandatory and vary widely in the practices covered (Ellefson *et al.* 1995). Although most program administrators consider mandatory regulations to be one of the least preferred program options (Kilgore and Blinn 2004, National Association of State Foresters 2001), regulatory programs do seem to be an effective way to achieve implementation of specified forest management practices (Henly *et al.* 1986).

A related development is the growth in non-State forest practices regulations in the form of forest certification systems. These voluntary systems are rapidly increasing in acreage and importance both in the United States and worldwide. They certify landowner compliance with a specified set of forest management procedures and practices. Although these systems are expected to continue to increase in importance, growth on NIPF lands is expected to trail that of other ownership types (Cashore *et al.* 2003).

Forest Landowner Cooperation

Although they have yet to reach a substantial number of landowners nationwide, examples of forest landowner cooperation are not hard to find. The Massachusetts Woodlands Cooperative (Barten *et al.* 2001) helps its NIPF owner members to obtain educational services, increased financial returns, access to equipment and professional expertise, and more. As we will learn in a later chapter, examples of forest landowner cooperation from other countries demonstrate that, in the right situations, these organizations can persist and provide value to their members.

Conclusions

The condition and trends across the United States describe a huge and widely dispersed population of small owners of a large land base. Collectively, the forest management decisions made by the members of this group will have important impacts on the availability of wood products for wood-using businesses. A diverse set of programs has been created to encourage active, sustainable forest management on NIPF lands. These programs have offered technical assistance, cost share payments, education, information, beneficial tax status, and other benefits, and the programs have had important impacts.

No single program can reach all landowners. Some studies (Bliss and Martin 1988, Egan 1997, Jones *et al.* 1995, Young and Reichenbach 1987) suggested that the forestry community's focus on the timber "problem" may prevent some programs from reaching landowners with different interests. Participation in a forest landowner cooperative provides a different opportunity for landowners to become engaged in their communities and to find local, trusted sources of information about forest management opportunities. Their potential to involve new landowners makes the trend in new cooperative development worthy of further attention. Whether, and for how long, large numbers of NIPF owners get involved in forest landowner cooperatives may determine the impact that these organizations will ultimately have.

Literature Cited

Alig, R.J.; Lee, K.J.; Moulton, R.J. 1990. Likelihood of timber management on nonindustrial private forests: evidence from research studies. Gen. Tech. Rep. SE-60. Asheville, NC: U.S. Department of Agriculture, Forest Service, Southeastern Forest Experiment Station. 17 p.

Barten, P.K.; Damery, D.; Catanzaro, P.; *et al.* 2001. Massachusetts family forests: birth of a landowner cooperative. Journal of Forestry. 99: 23-30.

Baughman, M.J.; Cervantes, J.C.; Rathke, D.M. 1998. Reaching Minnesota's nonindustrial private forest landowners. Unpublished report. St. Paul, MN: University of Minnesota. 5 p. [Available from author].

Birch, T.W. 1996. Private forest-land owners of the northern United States, 1994. Resour. Bull. NE-136. Radnor, PA: U.S. Department of Agriculture, Forest Service, Northeastern Forest Experiment Station. 293 p.

Bliss, J.C.; Martin, A.J. 1988. Identity and private forest management. Society and Natural Resources. 1: 365-376.

Bliss, J.C.; Martin, A.J. 1989. Identifying NIPF management motivations with qualitative methods. Forest Science. 35: 601-622.

Bullard, S.H.; Straka, T.J. 1988. Structure and funding of state-level forestry cost-share programs. Northern Journal of Applied Forestry. 5: 132-135.

Cashore, B.; Auld, G.; Newsom, D. 2003. Forest certification (eco-labeling) programs and their policy-making authority: explaining divergence among North American and European case studies. Forest Policy and Economics. 5: 225-247.

Cheng, A.S.; Ellefson, P.V. 1993. State programs directed at the forestry practices of private landowners: program administrators' assessment of effectiveness. Staff Pap. 87. St. Paul, MN: University of Minnesota, Department of Forest Resources. 35 p.

Cubbage, F.W.; New, B.D.; Moulton, R.J. 1996. Evaluations of technical assistance programs for nonindustrial private forest landowners. In: Baughman, M.J., ed. Symposium on nonindustrial private forests: learning from the past, prospects for the future. St. Paul, MN: University of Minnesota, Extension Special Programs, Minnesota Extension Service: 367-376.

Cubbage, F.W.; Risbrudt, C.D.; Skinner, T.M. 1987. Evaluating public forestry assistance programs: a case study in Georgia. Evaluation Review. 11: 33-49.

Cubbage, F.W.; Skinner, T.M.; Risbrudt, C.D. 1985. An economic evaluation of the Georgia Rural Forestry Assistance Program. Res. Bull. 322. Athens, GA: University of Georgia College of Agriculture Experiment Stations. 59 p.

Egan, A.F. 1997. From timber to forests and people: a view of nonindustrial private forest research. Northern Journal of Applied Forestry. 14: 189-193.

Egan, A.F. 1999. Reducing forest road erosion: do foresters and logging contracts matter? Journal of Forestry. 97: 36-39.

Egan, A.F; Gibson, D.; Whipkey, R. 2001. Evaluating the effectiveness of the Forest Stewardship Program in West Virginia. Journal of Forestry. 99: 31-36.

Ellefson, P.V.; Cheng, A.S.; Moulton, R.J.; University of Minnesota Agricultural Experiment Station. 1995. Regulation of private forestry practices by state governments. St. Paul, MN: University of Minnesota, Minnesota Agricultural Experiment Station.

Elwood, N.E.; Hansen, E.N.; Oester, P. 2003. Management plans and Oregon's NIPF owners: a survey of attitudes and practices. Western Journal of Applied Forestry. 18: 127-132.

Esseks, J.D.; Moulton, R.J. 2000. Evaluating the Forest Stewardship Program through a national survey of participating forest land owners. DeKalb, IL: Northern Illinois University, Center for Governmental Studies, Social Science Research Institute. 113 p.

Haynes, R.W.; Adams, D.M.; Mills, J.R. 1995. The 1993 RPA timber assessment update. Fort Collins, CO: U.S. Department of Agriculture, Forest Service, Rocky Mountain Forest and Range Experiment Station. 66 p.

Henly, R.K.; Ellefson, P.V.; Baughman, M.J.; University of Minnesota Agricultural Experiment Station. 1988. Minnesota's private forestry assistance program: an economic evaluation. St. Paul, MN: University of Minnesota, Minnesota Agricultural Experiment Station.

Henly, R.K.; Ellefson, P.V.; University of Minnesota Agricultural Experiment Station. 1986. State forest practice regulation in the United States: administration, cost, and accomplishments. St. Paul, MN: University of Minnesota, Minnesota Agricultural Experiment Station.

Jones, S.B.; Luloff, A.E.; Finley, J.C. 1995. Another look at NIPFs: facing our "myths." Journal of Forestry. 93: 41-44.

Kilgore, M.A.; Blinn, C.R. 2004. Policy tools to encourage the application of sustainable timber harvesting practices in the United States and Canada. Forest Policy and Economics. 6: 111-127.

Kline, J.D.; Azuma, D.L.; Alig, R.J. 2004. Population growth, urban expansion, and private forestry in western Oregon. Forest Science. 50: 33-43.

National Association of State Foresters. 2001. 2000 Progress report: State nonpoint source pollution control programs for silviculture. [Available on Internet: http://www.stateforesters.org/reports/NONPOINT%20REPORT.htm].

Row, C. 1978. Economies of tract size in timber growing. Journal of Forestry. 76: 576-582.

Royer, J.P. 1987. Determinants of reforestation behavior among southern landowners. Forest Science. 33: 654-667.

Skok, R.A.; Gregersen, H.M. 1975. Motivating private forestry: an overview. Journal of Forestry. 73: 202-205.

West, P.C.; Fly, J.M.; Blahna, D.J. 1988. The communication and diffusion of NIPF management strategies. Northern Journal of Applied Forestry. 5: 265-270.

Young, A.R.; Reichenbach, M.R. 1987. Factors influencing the timber harvesting intentions of nonindustrial private forest owners. Forest Science. 33: 381-393.

What is a Cooperative?

Kimberly Zeuli[1]

Groups of individuals throughout time have worked together in pursuit of common goals. The earliest forms of hunting and agriculture required a great deal of cooperation among humans. Although the word "cooperative" can be applied to many different types of group activities, in this publication it refers to a formal business model. Cooperative businesses are found in nearly all countries, in numerous and varied sectors of the economy. As Ivan Emelianoff (1942, 13), a respected cooperative scholar, once remarked, "the diversity of cooperatives is kaleidoscopic and their variability is literally infinite." As a consequence of this diversity, no universally accepted definition of a cooperative exists. Two definitions, however, are commonly used.

Figure 1.—*The "twin pines" is a familiar symbol for cooperatives in the United States. The Cooperative League of the USA, which eventually became the National Cooperative Business Association (NCBA), adopted it as their logo in 1922. The pine tree is an ancient symbol of endurance and immortality. The two pines represent mutual cooperation—people helping people.*

[1] Agriculture and Applied Economics, University of Wisconsin-Madison, zeuli@aae.wisc.edu

According to the International Co-operative Alliance (ICA), a cooperative is an autonomous association of persons united voluntarily to meet their common economic, social, and cultural needs and aspirations through a jointly owned and democratically controlled enterprise. Cooperative leaders around the world recognize the ICA, a non-governmental organization with more than 230 member organizations from more than 100 countries, as a leading authority on cooperative definition and values. The ICA definition recognizes the essential element of cooperatives: membership is *voluntary*. True cooperation with others arises from a belief in mutual help; it can't be coerced. In authentic cooperatives, people join voluntarily and have the freedom to quit the cooperative at any time. Therefore, the forced collectives prevalent in the former Soviet Union, for example, were not true cooperatives.

Another widely accepted cooperative definition is the one adopted by the U.S. Department of Agriculture (USDA) in 1987: a cooperative is a user-owned, user-controlled business that distributes benefits on the basis of use. This definition captures what are generally considered the three hallmarks of cooperatives: user-ownership, user-control, and proportional distribution of benefits. The "user-owner" principle implies that the people who use the co-op (members) help finance the co-op and, therefore, own the co-op. Members are responsible for providing at least some of the cooperative's capital. The equity capital contribution of each member should be in equal proportion to that member's use (patronage) of the co-op. This shared financing creates joint ownership. Cooperatives can certainly acquire debt capital, and in fact there are banks (such as CoBank and the National Cooperative Bank) that primarily loan to cooperatives. Typically, members generally contribute at least half of the capital in most cooperatives. They can contribute their share over time or when they join.

The "user-control" concept means that cooperative members govern their organization. They approve and amend the co-op's governing principles—the articles of incorporation and bylaws. They also elect a board of directors and must approve all mergers and any bankruptcy decisions. Cooperative state statutes and bylaws usually dictate that only active co-op members (those who use the co-op) are eligible to become voting directors, although nonmembers sometimes serve on boards in a non-voting, advisory capacity. Advisory directors are becoming more common in large agricultural cooperatives in the U.S., where complex financial and business operations require the expertise of financial and industry experts.

Voting rights are generally tied to membership status, usually one-member, one-vote, and not to the level of investment in or patronage of the cooperative. Cooperative law in a number of states in the U.S. and in other countries, however, also permits proportional voting. Instead of one vote per member, voting rights are based on the volume of business the member transacted the previous year with the cooperative. Generally, however, to prevent control by a minority of members, there is also a maximum number of votes any member may cast. For example, a grain cooperative might permit one vote to be cast for each 1,000 bushels of grain marketed the year before, but any single member would be limited to a maximum of 10 votes. Democratic control is maintained by tying voting rights to patronage. Equitable voting, or democratic control, is a quintessential attribute of cooperatives.

Cooperatives are bottom-up, not top-down organizations (fig. 2). Member control in a cooperative should not, however, extend into daily operations of the business. In most cooperatives, the board of directors hires a manager to take care of business. It is essential that the board understands the manager's (or management team's) responsibilities and does not try to micromanage the business. Therefore, it is important that care is taken in hiring a highly qualified, trustworthy individual as manager. The manager, the only employee that answers directly to the board, is responsible for carrying out the mission and vision of the cooperative, as established by the board of directors. In certain types of cooperatives—worker-owned or those managed as collectives—the members may also run the daily operations of the business.

"Distribution of benefits on the basis of use" is another key foundation for cooperatives. Members should share the benefits, costs, and risks of doing business in equal proportion to their patronage. The proportional basis is fair, easily explained (transparent), and entirely feasible from an operational standpoint. To do otherwise distorts the individual contributions of members and diminishes their incentives to join and patronize the cooperative.

Figure 2.—*Typical organization of a cooperative. (Source: Margaret Bau, USDA Rural Business Cooperative Service).*

Co-op benefits may include better prices for goods and services, improved services, and dependable sources of inputs and markets for outputs. Most cooperatives also realize annual net profits, all or part of which are returned to members in proportion to their patronage (thus, they are aptly called patronage refunds). Cooperatives also can return a portion of their profits as dividends on investment. In the U.S., however, Federal and most State statutes set an 8-percent maximum on annual dividend payments to ensure that the benefits of a cooperative accrue to those who use it most rather than to those who may have the most invested. Today, some co-op leaders and scholars consider this dividend restriction arbitrary and harmful to cooperatives. From their perspective, the 8-percent maximum makes investing in cooperatives less attractive than other forms of business. It makes cooperatives less competitive as well, especially in the agricultural processing sector, which requires a lot of capital for startup and growth.

In sum, cooperatives are organized to serve member needs and are focused on generating member benefits rather than returns to investors. This member-driven orientation makes them fundamentally different from other corporations. Additional cooperative structural characteristics and guiding principles further distinguish them from other business models. In most countries, the cooperative model represents only one of several different ways a business can choose to legally organize. One should consider many factors when choosing a business structure, including the liability of investors/owners, equity requirements, tax treatment, and ease/cost of business startup.

There are four basic categories of business in the U.S. (table 1). The sole proprietorship is the simplest, oldest, and most numerous of all types of business. One person owns and controls the enterprise. Partnerships involve at least two individuals. The primary downside of general partnerships and proprietorships is the unlimited liability: owners may lose not only their investment in the business, but also their other assets. The Limited Liability Company (LLC) is perhaps the most popular business form for multiple investors right now. It is a special type of partnership with a lot of flexibility and the limited liability status of other corporations. The fourth category includes all corporations. A cooperative is a special type of corporation, a subchapter T. The most predominant form of corporation (e.g., those traded on a public stock exchange) is the subchapter C. Any type of business can elect to be a nonprofit. Many people think of cooperatives as nonprofit enterprises, but this is incorrect. Most cooperatives in the U.S. are profit-oriented enterprises. However, unlike C-corporations, cooperatives return a portion or all of their profits to their members on the basis of their patronage rather than their investment levels.

Table 1.—*Basic business structures in the United States.*

Structure	Variation
Sole proprietorship	
Partnership	
Limited liability company (LLC)	
Corporation	Subchapter S
	Investor-owned firm (Subchapter C)
	Cooperative (Subchapter T)

Cooperatives in the U.S. Economy

Cooperatives exist in nearly every segment of our economy and have a significant economic impact. Cooperatives range in size from just a few employees in one small office, to very large firms with multinational operations. Most people are familiar with the large agricultural cooperative brand names such as Land O'Lakes in Minnesota, Cabot Creamery in Vermont, and Ocean Spray. Farmers create farm supply and marketing cooperatives to help them maximize their farms' net profits. This requires both effectively marketing their products for better prices as well as keeping input costs as low as possible. The farmers recognize they are more efficient and knowledgeable as producers than as marketers or purchasers. By selling and buying in larger volumes through a cooperative, they also can usually achieve better prices.

Consumer cooperatives are established to sell the products a group of consumers want but cannot find elsewhere at affordable prices. The consumer members are primarily interested in improving their purchasing power—the quantity of goods and services they can buy with their income. They naturally wish to get as much as possible for their money in terms of quantity and quality. As owners, the members have a say in what products their stores carry. Most people are probably familiar with local consumer food cooperatives, which often sell a whole range of grocery and health products, but often focus on natural or organic foods.

Rural utility cooperatives, created in the 1930s but now given a new image with the touchstone energy marketing campaign, credit unions, and health care cooperatives are also familiar to most of us. But cooperatives also exist in many other industries as well—ski resorts, newspapers, orchestras, funeral homes, and more. In some cases, these are worker-owned cooperatives. As the name suggests, a worker-owned cooperative is owned and controlled by its employees. Employees establish cooperatives in the hopes of increasing their wages and fringe benefits, improving their general working conditions, and ensuring job security.

Cooperatives play an important role in the American economy. About 48,000 cooperatives, operating in nearly every business sector imaginable, serve 120 million members, or roughly 4 out of 10 Americans (National Cooperative Business Association 2003a). The National Cooperative Bank keeps track of the top revenue generating cooperatives in America. Each co-op listed on its Co-op 100 index generated at least $346 million in revenue during 2002. Several cooperatives have been on the Fortune 500 list. The top 100 cooperatives in the U.S. generated, in the aggregate, $119 billion in 2002 (National Cooperative Business Association 2003b). They represent agriculture, finance, grocery, hardware, healthcare, recreation, and energy industries. Cooperatives are especially important to agriculture. In 2002, 3,140 agricultural cooperatives—with roughly 3.1 million farmer members (many farmers are members of more than one cooperative)—marketed and/or processed farm commodities, sold farm supplies, and provided other farm-related services. In 2001, they captured 28 percent of the market share of the cash value of products marketed by farmers and of the inputs purchased by farmers (Eversull 2004). In terms of nonagricultural cooperatives, 84 million Americans are members of 9,569 credit unions; 865 electric co-ops serve 37 million people in 47 States; more than 1.5 million families live in housing cooperatives; and more than 3 million people are members of 5,000 food cooperatives (Consumer Federation of America 2004, National Association of Housing Cooperatives 2004, National Rural Electric Cooperative Association 2004, United States Credit Union 2003).

Conclusions

When people think of cooperatives, they probably tend to think of their local consumer co-op or credit union or one of the large agricultural cooperatives. But cooperatives play a much broader role in our economy. It is therefore not surprising that people are rediscovering the cooperative model for applications in forestry.

Literature Cited

Consumer Federation of America. 2004. 2004 Statistics. [Available on Internet: http://consumerfed.org/backpage/coops.html#six].

Emelianoff, I. 1942. Economic theory of cooperation: economic structure of cooperative organizations. New York, NY: Columbia University. 279 p. Ph.D. dissertation.

Eversull, E.E. 2004. Farmer cooperative sales, incomes fall in 2002. Rural Cooperative Magazine. January/February: 28-29.

National Association of Housing Cooperatives. 2004. 2004 Statistics. [Available on Internet: http://www.coophousing.org/about_nahc.shtml].

National Cooperative Business Association (NCBA). 2003a. October 2003 Statistics. [Available on Internet: http://www.ncba.coop/abcoop_stats.cfm].

National Cooperative Business Association (NCBA). 2003b. Co-op 100 Statistics. [Available on Internet: http://www.co-op100.coop/coop100/indextop100.htm].

National Rural Electric Cooperative Asocation (NRECA). 2004. 2004 Statistics. [Available on Internet: http://nreca.coop/nreca/About_Us/Our_Members/Statistics/Statistics].

United States Credit Union. 2003. 2003 Statistics. [Available on Internet: http://www.cuna.org].

Cooperative Functions: Meeting Members' Needs

Mark G. Rickenbach[1]

Cooperatives are effective when they meet the needs of the members. In past and current offerings by cooperatives as a whole and forestry cooperatives in particular, four functional categories cover the typical services a forest landowner might gain access to through joining (Cobia 1989). The four categories—marketing, supply, service, and social—are defined and examples are provided.

Marketing

The marketing function of a cooperative is intended to increase the returns to members for forest products harvested from their land. By acting collectively in capturing economies of scale, private forest landowners receive greater profit than by acting alone. This collective action can, but does not have to, include value-added processing. While most foresters naturally think of timber products, landowner cooperatives also have been created around nontimber products such as maple syrup.

At the most basic level, the marketing function provides opportunities for the joint sale of timber. The co-op can organize several smaller sales that may be unprofitable as individual sales into a single, profitable sale as is commonly done by foresters in the private sector. If the co-op could predict wood supply from their members' lands over time, such knowledge might allow the co-op to negotiate long-term arrangements with local loggers or mills. Such knowledge may allow the co-op greater leverage in the marketplace to at least negotiate more favorable contracts, if not command higher prices.

Value-added processing can range from something as simple as a log sorting yard for the marketing of sawn logs to a sawmill or other facility that processes wood products for final sale to the public. However, entering the value-added wood products industry demands greater capital investments and greater attention to the factors that drive production. If members do not have wood available for the sawmill, where will the co-op get logs to keep the mill (and its employees) working? Even a log sorting yard can require careful consideration. Will the co-op buy or rent land? Will it harvest and haul the timber to the yard or will that work be contracted to others? Value-added processing can be an important part of a forest landowner cooperative: Sörda, the largest Swedish co-op, operates sawmills and paper mills.

We intend to market a product that has a story behind it, where we can tell people where the wood came from, how it was harvested, and where it was processed. We've been amazed at the wonderful reception we've been getting so far from people in this area.

Massachusetts Woodlands Cooperative Member

[1] Forest Ecology and Management, University of Wisconsin-Madison, mgrickenbach@wisc.edu

Supply

Rather than (or in addition to) marketing to external buyers, co-ops can help members by reducing the cost of supplies. In theory, a co-op can purchase supplies in bulk at prices lower than members purchasing by themselves. For example, agricultural co-ops purchase seed and fertilizers for their member farmers. In forestry, a co-op could purchase tree seedlings on behalf of all members and receive better prices for purchasing in bulk quantities. A co-op might also purchase equipment that could be shared by all members, but that would be impractical for individuals to purchase on their own, such as tree planters, pruning poles, or a firewood splitter.

Service

The service function includes those activities that are not strictly related to marketing or purchasing, but that still benefit members. Services might improve the profitability of individual members or the productivity of their forests. Many forestry co-ops assist members in developing written management plans, and they provide other technical assistance. The Sustainable Woods Cooperative of Lone Rock, WI, organized experts and members to burn prairies and oak savannahs to improve the qualities of those ecosystems. A co-op may retain or employ a forester or other professional to assist landowners with management activities. A co-op could also assist members by preparing applications to Federal or State cost share programs, overseeing members' participation in a forest certification system, or advising members on timber taxation issues.

The new co-ops have spent much effort in educating their members about forests and the practice of forestry. Co-ops, like others who work with forest landowners, have found that education is often the first step toward active forest management. This education has included everything from traditional forestry topics such as silviculture and timber marketing to ecological restoration and horse logging. The new co-ops also have used a variety of educational tools such as workshops, field days, publications, newsletters, and Internet sites. For co-ops, the educational service can be an important way of retaining members. Because forestry often requires only infrequent contact with members, educational programs can reconnect members with the co-op and remind them of the benefits it provides.

Social

Closely related to this reconnection through education is the social function that cooperatives play. Any group of people that interacts creates a social relationship. Several studies (Sturgess 2003, Tiles 2003) indicate that forest landowner co-ops bring together like-minded landowners with similar goals who gain much from their interaction with other members. Often, participation in the co-op further builds solidarity and like-thinking among members. However, these social benefits must be put in perspective. The decision to start or to participate in a co-op requires a full consideration of the costs and benefits, but the social benefits also can figure into an individual decision to join.

The thing I really like about cooperatives—there're other people there. You can call a half dozen landowners and say, "Hey, let me run this by you..." So, a cooperative is a resource that creates a continuous fabric. That's what I'm looking for.

Blue Ridge Forest Cooperative Potential Member

Conclusions

Forest landowner cooperatives can meet a variety of potential member needs ranging from marketing and supply arrangements to a wide range of professional and technical services. Through these cooperatives, members can create a social network of like-minded individuals. The selection of which needs to meet depends on a careful assessment of potential members and the existing market.

Literature Cited

Cobia, D.W., ed. 1989. Cooperatives in agriculture. London: Prentice Hall. 447 p.

Sturgess, E.D. 2003. Lumbering through lessons in landowner cooperation: a study of member perceptions of the Sustainable Woods Cooperative in southwestern Wisconsin. Madison, WI: University of Wisconsin, Department of Forest Ecology and Management. 91 p. M.S. thesis.

Tiles, K.A. 2003. Local landowner forestry groups and their members: what makes cooperation. Madison, WI: University of Wisconsin, Department of Forest Ecology and Management. 109 p. M.S. thesis.

Forestry Cooperatives: Past and Present

Mark G. Rickenbach[1]

Forest landowner cooperatives are not a new phenomenon, but past efforts to create and sustain these businesses have been largely unsuccessful in the U.S. Before and just after World War II saw significant investment in cooperative development that failed to create durable business. The purpose of this chapter is to briefly describe the history of forestry cooperatives in the U.S. and to provide a snapshot of co-ops today.

Checkered Past

An extensive literature review indicates that the first forestry co-ops in the U.S. were formed around the 1910s (Cunningham 1947). For example, the Rock Cooperative Company of Rock, MI, began in 1914. Solin (1940), in a case study of four forestry cooperatives in the Northeastern U.S., indicated that in upstate New York and New Hampshire co-ops were present as early as the 1920s. The Great Depression saw an increase in the number of co-ops with 57 in operation by 1944 (Cunningham 1947). In his review, Cunningham identified five categories—cooperative stores, marketing, processing, federations, and special purpose—of forestry co-ops based on the types of services (i.e., function) they provided their members (table 1). The largest and only processing co-op during this period was the Otsego Forest Products Cooperative of Cooperstown, NY (Inter-bureau Committee on Postwar Programs 1945), which had 950 members and annual sawtimber production of 2-3 million board feet.

Table 1.—*Forestry cooperatives in the United States, 1935–47 by functional category.*

Function	Number	Purpose and scope of activities
Cooperative store	3	Sold forest products for members (and sometimes for others) but were uninvolved with processing or forest management.
Marketing	30	Formed primarily for collective marketing of logs, pulpwood, and other timber products but strongly encouraged members to follow approved methods of logging and other forestry practices.
Processing	1	Processed members' timber.
Federation	11	Worked with local nonforestry cooperatives to conduct forest operations to provide members with lumber or wooden containers or to help them market timber products.
Special purpose cooperative	12	Formed to share forestry equipment and to market secondary forest products (e.g., Christmas trees, syrup).

Source: Cunningham 1947.

---

[1] Forest Ecology and Management, University of Wisconsin-Madison, mgrickenbach@wisc.edu

World War II and the postwar economic expansion were problematic for forestry co-ops. The Inter-bureau Committee on Postwar Programs (1945) identified several challenges to them, many "peculiar to cooperatives in the field of forestry" (p. 26). The report goes on…

Perhaps the most important is maintaining adequate control of timber cutting and other forest practices so as to keep the woodlands productive. There is little justification for any public support of marketing cooperatives that are not concerned with conservation of the forest resource. Another problem is how to maintain member interest when woodland operations are undertaken only at intervals of 3, 5, or 10 years rather than annually. A third problem is diversification of outlets for forest products so as to facilitate more complete utilization of the forest crop, improve growing stock, and make thinnings and other cultural practices profitable.

Still another problem, especially serious in cooperatives limited to marketing service, is getting members to sustain their output and live up to production commitments. The difficulty encountered on this is inherent in the fact that forestry is seldom the major concern of farmers and that there is no compelling time urgency for forest operations as with other crops. (p. 26-27)

Postwar cooperatives faced additional challenges including labor shortages, insufficient capital, competition from a growing forest products sector, and increased stumpage prices leading owners to deal directly with mills (Dempsey 1965). Amid these many challenges, forestry co-ops faded, but did not completely disappear.

Dempsey (1965) estimated that 20 co-ops remained in operation in 1965, and there was significant concern about their future. In that same year, Edward Grest, then Director of Cooperative Forest Management with the USDA Forest Service, addressed a forestry cooperative conference and asked attendees to avoid comparing current efforts to past failures (Grest 1965). To be clear, not all cooperatives during that period failed. For example, the Pertersham Forestry Cooperative Association was formed in 1938 to salvage timber from the 1938 hurricane. When the timber was salvaged, the co-op closed its doors. Nevertheless, the majority closed because they were unsuccessful.

As late as 1979, the number of forestry cooperatives was still small, seven by one account (Simon and Scoville 1982), and none survived through to the present day. Of these seven, none were formed before 1965.

Current Status

The late 1990s saw the resurgence of forest landowner cooperatives. Data from various sources (Smith and Sisock 2002, Tiles *et al.* 2004) indicate that 15-20 local forest landowner organizations are in various stages of development. Just over half are either cooperatives or organizations favoring that approach. The majority of the cooperatives are located in the Upper Midwest. Wisconsin has the most cooperatives and Minnesota and Iowa contribute several more. Other parts of the U.S., from the Pacific Northwest to the Northeast, also are seeing cooperatives form. The Southeast, at this point, has the fewest (Tiles *et al.* 2004).

Unlike previous efforts to form forest landowner cooperatives, current efforts have not relied substantially on direct public investment. The driving forces behind many current startups are nongovernmental organizations such as Cooperative Development Services (Madison, WI) and the Community Forest Resource Center (Minneapolis, MN) and landowners themselves. Also, the current emphasis has been on ecologically sustainable forest practices instead of past emphases such as economic development and timber supply. Often this emphasis on sustainable practices includes forest certification.

As was noted, landowners are a driving force in the current cooperative movement. While membership is defined by each co-op, anecdotal evidence suggests that landowners are the only members. Loggers and small-scale processors can also be found in modern forest landowner co-ops.

Learning from the Past

Given the checkered, but well-documented past of forestry cooperatives in the U.S., review of past literature, particularly those publications that have a "how-to" focus (Dempsey 1968, Dempsey and Markeson 1969, Hoffman 1985, Markeson 1965, USDA 1967), can provide information for current efforts. These publications distill success or at least attribute success to three factors: (1) get the numbers right, (2) complete an inventory before formation, and (3) ensure member commitment for the long term.

Get the Numbers Right
Cooperatives are fundamentally businesses. For a business to be successful, its costs and expected returns must provide acceptable returns to investors. Although most owners do not look to their land to provide significant income, they also do not want to throw money away. Landowners, like everyone else, want to know what they are in for when they join something, and the finances are a big part of that.

Complete an Inventory
It is important to understand the forest resource upon which the cooperative is built. Knowing how many owners with how much land tells a great deal about the types of services and amount of time that might be required. Such data are essential in setting a

In order to succeed you need two very important factors. You need to produce a good product. You also need consumers. You need to notify potential local consumers, people who drive by your land who have no idea what you're doing. You need to have them understand the importance of buying local products.

Massachusetts Woodlands Cooperative Member

cost and fee structure that reflects the operational reality of the cooperative. If value-added processing is to be a primary service of the cooperative, detailed inventory and harvest schedule data are essential to determining the likely success of a processing facility.

Ensure Member Commitment

It is essential that the cooperative have members that are committed to its success. The best way to do this is to create a cooperative that reflects the needs, interests, and values of the members. With forest landowners and their often varied ownership objectives, this can be easier said than done. Yet, to remain a viable cooperative over the long term, member commitment is essential.

Conclusion

Cooperatives are not a new phenomenon in the U.S., but they have a checkered past often marked by failure. The current effort to create forestry cooperatives would do well to build on the lessons of previous attempts. Specifically, new and forming forest landowner cooperatives should carefully evaluate the costs and benefits to members, build these estimates on accurate inventories of the forest resources, and maintain a committed membership. Even after following this advice, the cooperative may fail, but it is sure to do so if these lessons are ignored.

Literature Cited

Cunningham, R.N. 1947. Forestry cooperatives in the United States. USDA Forest Service Report 6. Washington, DC: U.S. Department of Agriculture, Forest Service. 18 p.

Dempsey, G.P. 1965. A review of forest-based cooperatives. In: Forestry cooperatives: workshop proceedings; 1965 September 14-15; Denver, CO. Washington, DC: USDA Committee on Forestry: 49-61.

Dempsey, G.P. 1968. Some new guidelines for the forest cooperative. Journal of Forestry. 66(1): 17-21.

Dempsey, G.P.; Markeson, C.B. 1969. Guidelines for establishing forestry cooperatives. Res. Pap. NE-133. Upper Darby, PA: U.S. Department of Agriculture, Forest Service, Northeastern Forest Experiment Station. 38 p.

Grest, E.G. 1965. Objectives of workshop. In: Forestry Cooperatives: workshop proceedings; 1965 September 14-15; Denver, CO: 1965 April 20-21; Princeton, WV. Washington DC: USDA Committee on Forestry cooperatives.

The members were a select group. They were landowners and most had some history where they had seen really poor forestry practices, and they thought something could be done better.

Sustainable Woods Cooperative Member

Hoffman, B.F., Jr. 1985. Estimating production of forest cooperative members. Res. Rep. 45. Washington, DC: U.S. Department of Agriculture, Agricultural Cooperative Service. 34 p.

Inter-bureau Committee on Postwar Programs. 1945. Agricultural cooperatives in the postwar period. Washington, DC: U.S. Department of Agriculture. 41 p.

Simon, D.M.; Scoville, O.J. 1982. Forestry cooperatives: organization and performance. Res. Rep. 25. Washington, DC: U.S. Department of Agriculture, Agricultural Cooperative Service. 24 p.

Smith, D.; Sisock, M. 2002. Distribution of existing forestry cooperatives in the United States. In: 9th International symposium on society and resource management; 2002 June 2-5; Bloomington, IN. [Unpublished paper].

Solin, L. 1940. A study of farm woodland cooperatives in the United States. Bulletin of the New York State College of Forestry Tech. Pub. 48. Syracuse, NY: New York State College of Forestry. 118 p.

Tiles, K.A.; Rickenbach, M.G.; Sturgess, E.D.; Zeuli, K. 2004. U.S. forest landowner cooperatives: What do members expect? What can cooperatives deliver? In: Baumgartner, D.M., ed. Human dimensions of family, farm, and community forestry; 2004 March 29-April 1; Pullman, WA. Pullman, WA: Washington State University Extension: 135, 138.

USDA. 1967. Proceedings of Forestry Cooperatives Workshops, 1967. Proceedings of workshops held in Atlanta, GA; Columbus, OH; and Salt Lake City, UT during 1967. 43 p.

Forest Owner Cooperation Around the World:
Where, How, and Why It Succeeds

David B. Kittredge[1]

The cooperation of private forest owners appears to be enjoying a renaissance of interest in the United States. The success of the national satellite conference on the subject is just one indication of new popularity, or a need to know more. Small, locally based efforts are springing up in a number of states, and a certain momentum has built in the last 5-10 years. As described by Rickenbach in an earlier chapter, this is apparently not the first time there has been interest like this in the United States. Groups of private landowners have experimented with different types of cooperation over the years, but they have not withstood the test of time. As a result, to some, this current interest may appear new. Private forest owners in other countries have cooperated for decades and continue to do so, however, and many examples have proven to be both durable and productive.

In 2002, I sought examples of private forest owner cooperation from around the world to determine the extent of this activity and look for common causes or themes central to its success. I intentionally limited my search to countries with developed economies and relatively high standards of living. There are many examples of cooperation on a subsistence or community basis from developing nations, but I wanted to find examples that would be applicable in the United States, where private forest owners are relatively affluent and do not generally depend on their woodlands for subsistence income. I also sought examples from temperate countries that have forest growth rates roughly equivalent to those in the United States. Cooperation might work well in tropical countries with rapid forest growth rates, but I wanted to find examples that would be relevant to the forest conditions more typical of the U.S. climate.

My search for information involved several different techniques. I conducted a comprehensive review of the published forestry literature that went back to 1988. I also conducted an Internet search of applicable Web sites. In addition, I e-mailed more than 150 Extension Forestry professionals from around the world who participate in the International Union of Forestry Research Organizations' Extension Working Group. I requested leads, contacts, or other information about private forest owner cooperation in their countries. Finally, I had the good fortune to be able to travel to Sweden for 2 weeks and visit four of the largest private forest owner cooperatives and learn firsthand about their success. I cannot claim that my search was comprehensive or that I succeeded in finding all examples. Information about cooperatives may not make it into

[1] Department of Natural Resources Conservation, University of Massachusetts, Amherst, MA, dbk@forwild.umass.edu

the published forestry literature, which often focuses on research results. I may not have found everything there is on the Internet, or I may have been thwarted by a language barrier. I believe my results provide a strong indication of the extent and nature of private forest owner cooperation internationally, but I am equally certain that I missed some excellent examples. Because my search was limited to written materials, I may not have gathered all the fine details of how these organizations function, a full understanding of which would come from a personal visit. Lastly, my search uncovered no other similar review.

Results

Where

In the broadest sense, I found evidence of private forest owner cooperation from more than 19 countries (Australia, Austria, Belgium, Canada, Finland, Sweden, Denmark, Germany, France, Japan, South Korea, Switzerland, Netherlands, United Kingdom, Ireland, New Zealand, Norway, Lithuania, Slovenia). It is very hard to estimate the total numbers of owners who cooperate, since that cooperation can take different forms. Also, a single "member" or participant may be an organization like a church or local community, composed itself of members. I broadly estimate that more than 3.6 million private forest owners are involved in some form of cooperation, and the total area of affected forest land exceeds 28.3 million ha.

I found more than 300 descriptions of cooperative organizations in temperate countries with developed economies. Although the levels of cooperation vary, millions of private owners work together to achieve results they believe are superior to what they could do independently. Cooperation for some may be merely working together on a newsletter or otherwise exchanging information, but for many others it represents working together and marketing millions of cubic meters of wood annually. Although cooperation may be viewed as a re-emerging fad among some owners in the United States, it has succeeded for decades elsewhere.

How

I found a wide variety of different forms and degrees of cooperation, which could be broken down into four types: information, equipment, financial, management.

Figure 1.—*Japanese forest owners who are part of a cooperative discuss silvicultural options for a Japanese larch stand. (Photo credit: D. Kittredge).*

Information Cooperation

Information, techniques, experiences, and advice are exchanged among owners, but cooperation does not extend to actual land management or marketing. These organizations or associations disseminate and exchange information through a variety of means, such as workshops, meetings, trips, newsletters, market reports, advice, and "advocacy" of private owner interests in State or Federal policy activities. Examples of this type of cooperation can be found in most countries.

Equipment Cooperation

Participating landowners share equipment and machinery for road building and access and for harvesting/transport, but their lands are managed independently of one another. Equipment cooperation is practiced in the Canadian provinces of Quebec, New Brunswick, and Nova Scotia as well as in Finland and Slovenia.

Figure 2.—*Forester for Swedish forest owners cooperative poses with operator of a small harvester in a dense Scotch pine stand. (Photo credit: D. Kittredge).*

Financial Cooperation

This type of cooperation involves members who collectively market wood products to gain a better position in the marketplace. This is common in Scandinavia, where large organizations with thousands of owners negotiate strong prices with industrial buyers of roundwood. This model is also found in Japan, South Korea, eastern Canadian provinces, Germany, and Austria.

These organizations generally operate on the cooperative principle of one-member-one-vote. Members purchase and own shares, the number of which is often based on the size of their property. They earn annual dividends, value growth of their shares, or profits when the "company" has a successful year. In comparison, private corporations return profits to stockholders rather than to forest owners. Industrial roundwood buyers strive to minimize the price paid for wood to maximize profits for stockholders. Negotiations between the cooperative organizations and buyers of roundwood generally result in higher overall prices in the marketplace. Thus, members benefit when they sell wood, and they benefit from a return on their shares as the value of those shares grows. In some cases, these organizations are not exclusive, and they will buy wood from nonmembers, as well.

Over time, many of these organizations have realized the gains of capturing "value-added" benefits and now do more than simply negotiate the sale of roundwood. Many have added sawmill capacity, and one cooperative in southern Sweden has even built its own pulp mill.

Figure 3.—*Forester for Swedish forest owners cooperative uses his cell phone to make contact with roundwood buyers. (Photo credit: D. Kittredge).*

Figure 4.—*Forest owners cooperative in southern Germany deals not only in conventional wood products, but also in pelletized wood for home heating. (Photo credit: D. Kittredge).*

Many of these organizations do not limit themselves to wood transactions. They offer members many other benefits, such as information and educational opportunities, and advocacy representation. They also offer the benefits of economies of scale to purchase in large quantities and pass savings for goods and services on to members. Several of these organizations have evolved to further offer land management services to members generally on a fee-for-service basis. They either do this in-house with their own staff or refer members to independent contractors. Many urban absentee owners, who often live some distance from their property, welcome this "full service" opportunity. This is actually a growing trend in Scandinavia, Japan, and eastern Canada, and this "consignment" or "absentee" management role is anticipated to grow.

Management Cooperation

Although participants in financial cooperation organizations collaborate for a better position in the marketplace, they do not necessarily cooperate in a true integrated management sense, making decisions on similar spatial and temporal scales and in context of their surroundings. This kind of "ecosystem-based approach to management" seems quite rare, although the activities of Landcare groups in Australia seem to approach this. There are examples of owners who cooperate in management, but not in a necessarily integrated way at larger ecosystem scales.

Examples of the different types of cooperatives are shown in table 1.

Table 1.—*Examples of different types of cooperation in the forestry sector found outside the United States.*

Resources being shared			
Information	**Equipment**	**Financial**	**Management**
• Lobbying or political activity and advocacy • Sharing knowledge and peer experiences (e.g., compare experiences with a given contractor, which would be impossible for public sector foresters to fairly or ethically do) • Information and educational opportunities	• Share equipment or contractors for a particular task • Road construction, access, and maintenance tasks	• Purchase supplies or insurance in bulk, thereby gaining a better price • Purchase professional services, such as boundary work, surveys, or management planning • Collective marketing of wood • Financial assistance (e.g., South Korean owners may take out loans from their local cooperative) • Assemble a sufficient volume of land and owners to participate in some form of green certification • Develop regional recognition or a "brand" for wood products, and potentially greater value • Due to economies of scale, attain greater access to government and private sector grants (e.g., the Landcare group experiences in Australia)	• Fire detection, fuel reduction, and response • Joint recreation and habitat planning, access, and lease opportunities • Promotion and organization of afforestation or reforestation efforts • Ecosystem-level services (e.g., avalanche protection in mountainous regions such as Switzerland and Japan) • Management services for absentee landowners • Consolidation of very small parcels in fragmented landscapes to assemble an effective management unit (e.g., groupings of parcels in France, Germany, and the Netherlands)

Why

In basically all circumstances, government was involved in the development of cooperative groups. These organizations are considered a means to implement national forest policy or safeguard public benefits on private lands. In Nova Scotia, for example, government funding supported the creation of a cooperative, and members used creative entrepreneurial ideas to succeed beyond the initial supported phase. In Belgium, the Netherlands, France, Germany, and Japan, governments financially support cooperatives, where they are an effective tool to promote forest management on private lands. This support is delivered either directly through payments to the organization, or indirectly, routing subsidies for landowner management through the organization, which takes an overhead share. Some governments actually pay landowners directly to join their local cooperative organization (e.g., France, Netherlands). State and Federal

Figure 5.—*Foresters for a Swedish forest owners cooperative on a landing with wood sold to a local buyer. (Photo credit: D. Kittredge).*

programs in the United States promote good forestry on private lands through direct cost sharing of activities and provision of technical assistance through public-sector county foresters. In contrast, other counties view the role of successful cooperative organizations as worthy of public investment and as a means to promote good forestry on private lands.

In all cases, cooperation of private landowners was in response to some issue or stimulus. In Scandinavia, low prices and a lack of competition inspired landowners to bargain collectively for a higher roundwood price. A similar interest in negotiating from a position of strength led owners in the Canadian Maritime provinces to cooperate. The need for fuelwood in Scandinavia during World War II called for an efficient means of production and distribution.

A need for reforestation in rural areas moved the South Korean government to form Village Forestry Associations. Likewise, the need for reforestation on private lands led the Québec Provincial government to work with cooperatives. Later, when a need for local woodsworker training and recruiting surfaced, cooperatives were seen as a good approach. In the UK and the Netherlands, the need to restore native broadleaved woodlands inspired nature conservancy organizations and the government to form cooperative organizations. Similarly in Australia, concern over environmental degradation inspired local volunteer groups to collaborate with government and industry through Landcare programs.

Some woodland owners in British Columbia sought an alternative to either the large-scale industrial or provincial approach to forestry and instead started organizations for information, education, and support. Such organizations can provide a means to pursue some form of green certification.

The continued hyper-fragmentation of land into tiny parcels through inheritance motivated government officials and foresters in France, Belgium, parts of Germany, and the Netherlands to start cooperative organizations. In southern Germany, for example, average ownership size can be 10 acres or less, distributed between two or three different parcels. Any kind of effective management or care of these tiny properties requires efficiencies of cooperation.

The development of overstocked or newly established conifer plantations in need of tending, as well as a market for small wood, inspired governments or landowners to seek cooperative means to promote action on private lands in Japan, Ireland, and parts of the UK.

Hundreds of examples and success stories from 19 different countries attest to the effectiveness of cooperation. Many of these have withstood the test of time, prospering for 50 years or more. These organizations, in spite of impressive track records, are not universally appealing to all owners, however. For example, Finnish landowners are legally required to contribute to associations, but only 75 percent of them actually participate in them. Thousands of Swedish owners participate in a cooperative, but this still represents only roughly half the NIPF owner population. Approximately two-thirds of Japanese owners, and three-fourths of forest land are enrolled in a cooperative. Roughly a quarter of the landowners and two-thirds of the forest are enrolled in a cooperative in the southern German state of Bavaria. Even where cooperation is very successful, it is not universally accepted. Clearly individual owners have their own reasons for participating in cooperatives, or deciding not to.

Conclusions

This review reveals hundreds of examples of forest owner cooperation at a non-subsistence level from temperate countries around the world. Thousands of owners and millions of hectares are involved. Cooperation ranges from a simple exchange of information to sophisticated business transactions annually involving millions of cubic meters. Although the nature and extent of cooperation vary, both private owners and governments deem the outcomes beneficial. In virtually all examples, there was some level of public sector involvement, at least in the early stages, and a cause or stimulus that prompted a cooperative response. This review cannot be considered exhaustive or to represent all forms of cooperation worldwide. It does provide a good indication of the relative success of cooperation in other countries similar to the United States. Although cooperation in these countries may not enjoy universal appeal, it is an integral part of the success of forestry.

Achieving Cooperative Success[1]

Kimberly Zeuli[2]

Success of a cooperative depends on the foundation built during its organization. Successful businesses are not started overnight. Careful and deliberate planning must be started long before the co-op opens its doors. This chapter begins with an outline of six fundamental steps that should be followed when organizing any cooperative. From initial concept to the start of operations, this process may take anywhere from 6 months to several years. This outline is followed by excerpts from interviews with three forestry cooperative resource professionals: Paul Catanzaro, Katie Fernholz, and E.G. Nadeau. They share their insights into the roles such professionals play in forestry co-op development. Finally, this chapter ends with a summary of the lessons they have learned in establishing successful cooperatives.

Steps for Organizing a Cooperative

Step 1: Determine the Need for the Co-op

The first step is the most essential. Co-ops should be organized only in response to a specific problem or an opportunity identified by a group. Viable cooperatives are usually initiated by a small group of people who share a common problem or see some opportunity they can capture by working together. They jointly decide what the cooperative will do. Often this group becomes the co-op's steering committee. The steering committee puts in a lot of time and effort in developing the co-op committee. The committee has four general responsibilities:

1. Direct the preparation of a feasibility study
   - Find a reputable and experienced person or firm to prepare the study
   - Compare business models
2. Prepare a business plan that defines the co-op's operations and requirements for success
   - Find a reputable and experienced person or firm to prepare the plan
3. Present results from the feasibility study and business plan to other potential members
4. Determine whether to proceed or not with the co-op development

[1] The author wishes to thank Margaret Bau, a Cooperative Development Specialist at USDA Rural Development in Wisconsin, for her insightful comments.

[2] Agriculture and Applied Economics, University of Wisconsin-Madison, zeuli@aae.wisc.edu

Step 2: Hold an Exploratory Meeting

If group members are able to decide on a joint business idea, they need to hold an exploratory meeting with other potential members to gauge their interest in the idea. Is there sufficient interest? If not, the organizational efforts may stop here. Perhaps the group can look into other business models such as LLCs or Partnerships that require less support. The advantages and disadvantages of the cooperative model should be discussed at this meeting. Co-ops require time and money from each member. At this meeting the typical member should learn what will be expected from him or her, both in the short term and well into the future.

A great way to ensure member commitment is to ask the participants for their time and for some seed money to help with the ongoing organizational effort. Some people at the meeting also should be willing to serve on a steering committee to help bring the idea to the next level.

Step 3: Determine If the Co-op Is a Feasible Business Idea

Feasibility studies, no matter how good, are only expectations. They do not guarantee success. If the study is positive, the steering committee then proceeds to create a business plan. Typically, it takes 1.5-2 years to organize a cooperative. Researching and writing a feasibility study and business plan are by far the most time consuming tasks in co-op development. Often, people feel projects lose their momentum at this stage. But it is critical for potential co-ops to do their homework before asking members to invest hard-earned money and resources.

Step 4: Incorporate

If, after completing the feasibility study and business plan, the steering committee members decide to proceed, they need to incorporate their business. This is an appropriate time to consult a lawyer, if one hasn't already been consulted. All businesses need to incorporate with their state. If the organization is a co-op, the co-op typically has to write the bylaws, essentially an owner's manual for the co-op. Bylaws state how the co-op will be governed and how it will conduct business.

Step 5: Raise Sufficient Capital

The most challenging step for businesses is usually raising adequate capital. This can be more of a challenge for cooperatives because, as mentioned by Sagor, the members provide a substantial amount of the capital. For capital-intensive ventures, this may be sufficient reason for a group to choose a different business structure. For example, if the group decides it wants to build a timber mill, which costs a few million dollars, it may not be able to finance that solely with member capital and bank loans. It may decide to become an LLC or a publicly traded company to access some venture capital. If a group wants less capital-intensive services, such as forest management or education, raising member equity is less of an issue.

Step 6: Get Started!

A few things need to get done to get the co-op off and running on the right track. At the first meeting, the members approve the co-op bylaws and elect a board of directors. Finding great board members is really essential. Finding the right initial manager is also critical. Then there are the details of finding the right facilities, of the manager hiring other staff, and getting operations under way.

The Role of the Resource Professional: Discussions with Paul Catanzaro, Katie Fernholz, and E.G. Nadeau

There is much to learn from people who have experience in organizing and running a forest landowner cooperative. We interviewed three resource professionals who have worked in the area for a number of years. Paul Catanzaro is a service forester in the Bureau of Forestry under the Massachusetts Department of Conservation and Recreation, and in that capacity he provides technical assistance to private landowners and land trust towns. He is also a regulator and implements the Massachusetts Forest Cutting Practices Act as well as the State's current use program (Chapter 61).

Katie Fernholz is a forester at the Community Forestry Resource Center (CFRC), a program of the Institute for Agriculture and Trade Policy (IATP) in Minneapolis, MN.[3] Katie has worked at CFRC since 1999 and has helped support the development of more than a dozen landowner groups and cooperatives in the Upper Midwest. Katie also has helped facilitate co-op development in other parts of the country through sharing her experiences and the lessons learned in the Midwest. Katie's specific tasks with cooperative development efforts have primarily been related to helping landowners realize their forest management goals. By arranging educational opportunities, field days, and workshops, Katie has helped co-op members learn more about land management options and tools they can use to achieve their goals. Katie also has helped many of the groups with their goal of having their forests certified. Katie helped establish CFRC's Umbrella Certification Program that provides co-op members and other family forests in the Upper Midwest access to Forest Stewardship Council (FSC) certification through an innovative group certification structure and enrollment process.

E.G. Nadeau is the director of research, planning and development for Cooperative Development Services (CDS). E.G. has more than 20 years of cooperative development experience, including 7 years working with forestry co-ops and associations. He is the

---

[3] Katie left CFRC in June 2004 and is now at Dovetail Partners in White Bear Lake, MN.

national coordinator of WoodWorks, a network of seven cooperative development centers interested in forest owner cooperation.

We start with Paul and move on to learn from Katie and E.G.

How did you originally get involved with the Massachusetts Woodland Cooperative?
Paul: I originally got involved with the Massachusetts Woodland Cooperative because of a need I identified in my daily routine as a service forester. It became increasingly difficult to watch landowners implement management which did not achieve their goals. Either the work they were getting wasn't up to their standards or they were making resource decisions based on misinformation. This has huge implications when the landscapes are dominated by nonindustrial private landowners. It jeopardizes the public good that flows from these lands. In response, several other resource professionals and I decided to get together and propose the forestry co-op idea to several landowners in the area as a way of helping landowners achieve their goals while at the same time raising the standard of management in the area and protecting the public benefits that private forests provide.

In the summer of 1999 I had conversations with the state's extension forester, Dave Kittredge, as well as another professor at U Mass, Paul Barten, about the idea of gathering some landowners together to take a look at getting the group certified. Was it even possible? Paul Barten and I talked to other resource professionals in the fall of 1999, and we all threw into the hat the names of landowners we knew that may be open to exploring this idea. We organized a meeting of landowners and resource professionals in October 1999. The landowners expressed interest in pursuing the idea. We then began meeting every month for approximately 3 or 4 years.

My involvement with the cooperative in its startup phases moved very quickly from one of being an organizer to one of being a resource professional giving technical assistance. Originally, it was a group of resource professionals that organized the first several meetings, identified some key landowners in our target area, and invited them to a meeting and presented them with the co-op idea. We all agreed that for this initiative to be successful, it needed to be landowner driven with support from resource professionals. Unlike many traditional forestry programs where landowners are passive participants, we all felt that one of the important outcomes would be a group of empowered landowners. It was important to move from leader to technical support as quickly as possible. Indeed, within two to three meetings, landowners were comfortable and excited enough to start running the meetings and provide direction for the cooperative.

At our original meeting, we invited 20 to 25 landowners and by the second or third meeting we had probably close to 15; several had dropped out but several new landowners had heard of the meeting and really wanted to attend. So we have been working primarily with somewhere around 15 dedicated landowners.

Today, the group has formally organized legally as an LLC with cooperative bylaws. The LLC has obtained Green Certification through FSC and is in the process of developing a business plan.

So what is your role today? How much time do you still devote to this project?
Paul: Early in the process we received a $40,000 grant from the Forest Service through its Focus Funding Project, which we used as seed money to help with this initiative. As part of that grant, I used a portion of my time as a match (an in-kind contribution), devoting an average of 5 hours a week for the 2-year life of the grant. My match for the grant was spent providing technical assistance for the fledgling effort. The cooperative is now at a point where I'm giving approximately 5 hours a month, and I have moved from being an organizer to primarily working with the landowners on their FSC Green Certification.

One of the things, especially early on, that I found very helpful in my work with the cooperative was being able to provide some stability during the fits and the starts of the startup phase as landowners got tired or something discouraging happened. In the future, I envision my role as one of continued technical assistance and support.

And what about you, Katie and E.G., what experiences have you had with forestry cooperatives?
Katie: I think the role of anyone who's trying to assist in co-op development, whatever their background experience might be, is to facilitate and empower the local group, to help them articulate and pursue whatever their ideas are. So it's a very delicate process because even if the development specialist has a lot of experience and can see all of the things that the group should be doing and whatnot, it's very important that they go only at the pace that the group is capable of. You have to step back and let the local people who are the members of the co-op run the show and you step in when they really need help, when they are kind of getting bogged down in something or when they ask for help, but not lead it, not push it, and not force it to be something that it doesn't want to be. The strength of any co-op project is the local ownership, the local investment. That's what will keep the project going when the co-op development specialists go away.
E.G.: We do a whole range of things to help existing co-ops and to work with people who are interested in forming co-ops. We do everything from facilitating initial planning meetings, to writing business plans, to doing market studies, to helping groups secure financing for their projects.

When do you generally get involved in the process?
Katie: Co-op development specialists or assistants can come in at a variety of stages throughout a project. Some communities have a culture that says right from the beginning they want to pull in as many people as possible so they'll invite a wide range of people to the very first visioning meetings. Other communities have a culture that says no, we

Well, the benefit of having loggers, foresters, processors, and landowners come together in a co-op is one of basic familiarity. When people come together over and over and over again, they get to know each other, and they understand and respect each other.

Massachusetts Woodland Cooperative Member

first have to get our own footing and identify for ourselves what our boundaries are and our goals are, and once we're secure in that then we will bring in other people when we get to specific questions or needs. So, in my experience, it depends on the culture of the community.

E.G.: Cooperative development specialists can be brought into a co-op development process at a variety of different stages. We can be involved at the very first organizing meeting where a co-op idea is being discussed all the way to working with a co-op that has been in existence for 50 years and assisting the leadership to carry out a strategic planning review.

How do you measure the interest of potential cooperative members?
Katie: The interest level for co-op development in a community or among potential members can be measured very formally through surveys. I think every group I've been involved with has done an initial survey of landowners within their region. They usually identify a watershed or a county or a multiple county area and get a list of the various landowners and just do a blanket mailing. The response to that gives some indication of what the interest level is.

More informally, interest level can be gauged just by how enthusiastically the people respond to the idea. I mean, most groups do have a first meeting and at the end of that first meeting you'll have kind of a show of hands of who thinks we should keep going with this. I remember one meeting I was at, it was a broad informational meeting; people were going to present on co-op experiences from other groups and it was a pretty full room, maybe 100 or a 150 landowners from a couple of counties in that area. It was really hard to tell during that meeting what was going to happen because there weren't a lot of questions; the audience was kind of tight-lipped and arms were crossed and you weren't quite sure if they were into it or not. But at the end of the meeting, they were asked whether they thought this was a good idea. Every hand went up. Sometimes you've just got to ask.

E.G.: A professional consultant like me can't really determine for a group whether or not they have a good idea for a co-op. We can work with a group or with a co-op and explore together whether it makes sense to proceed with a business based on their idea. One thing that can be very useful is to do a survey of potential members of a local co-op. In the forestry co-ops that we've been working with around the Midwest, one of the steps that we almost always recommend is to contact local landowners who might be interested in joining the co-op. Ask them if they are interested in receiving forestry services from the co-op. If so, what kinds of services do they want? This should be a key initial decision-making point on whether or not to proceed with the development of the co-op.

If you don't do a member survey when a co-op or association is being formed, the organizing group can head off in a direction that is different from what potential members want. In fact, I can think of one critical example where the organizers did do a membership survey and then didn't follow it. The membership survey showed that people were very interested in education and in receiving forest management services, and not very interested in marketing their timber or creating value-added products. And yet, the co-op leaders made value-added wood processing their priority activity. So it's not just a matter of doing the survey, you also have to pay attention to the results.

How do you initially get members involved?
Katie: To get members involved in the beginning, one of the best strategies I've seen is to simply do a field day, a workshop, or a walk in the woods that is focused around what is perceived to be an important issue in the area. Holding an informal workshop and inviting people from the area helps identify what people have in common and who might be the leaders in that community.

E.G.: There's no magic formula for how to start one of these things. There are some cautions about what not to do, though. One caution is that you don't just keep having open-ended meetings. You have maybe one open-ended meeting. Then you pick a steering committee. Then the steering committee creates an action plan and follows the action plan. If you have a series of open-ended meetings and anybody who wants to can come and talk about whatever they want, it becomes like the movie "Groundhog Day." Every meeting is a variation on the same theme that is played out again and again and again. People get discouraged and think they are wasting their time and stop coming.

What about bringing in other resource professionals?
Katie: Co-ops in early development stages can benefit from bringing in outside financial expertise at a variety of stages. Some groups worry about the numbers and the dollar signs very early in the process, and they really want to get down into the financial nitty-gritty as soon as possible. But I think the financial expertise can be brought in at a variety of stages. I do think that finance is one area where external expertise is the most important. When it comes to really having enough experience with the numbers, unless the board members are personally experienced in their other lives at doing business planning or financial forecasts, it is an area where outside third parties and financial experts become critical.

All kinds of different experts can blend information and experience at the various co-op development stages. For any co-op, every time a question comes up in a meeting, it's appropriate to say, 'is there someone else that would know more about this?' They should make sure that it is someone that they trust, that they trust to both provide them good information and also to be respectful of any requests they have for privacy about

Forestry is getting to be a very complex business these days. You've got to have foresters, you've got to have business people, you need to have money people, legal people, biologists, "-ologists," the whole ball of wax. I really think that one of the strengths of a cooperative is being able to draw together a very wide, diverse professional set of resource professionals to make the whole thing work.

Lewis County, Washington, Potential Cooperative Member

their process and about the debates they are having. Various forestry co-ops have certainly benefited from the engagement of resource managers, foresters, ecologists, and loggers—all kinds of people working through the whole range of the forest products industry.

E.G.: It's very important to talk to a lawyer when you are developing your bylaws and deciding on the kind of business you want to form. One thing that you have to be careful of though is not to bring an attorney in too quickly. Attorneys are expensive. So, my advice is to get a pretty good idea of the direction you want to go with your organization and then consult an attorney and find out if there are any major reasons why you should or should not go in the direction you have decided. If you follow that approach, you can get good legal advice without having to invest a lot of money in it.

A number of very good forestry professionals can be helpful at different stages in the formation of a forest co-op or association. They include State foresters, and forestry staff located around States. They include private consulting foresters, loggers, extension staff, and staff of local resource conservation and development districts. All these people are potentially valuable resource people in forming an organization. In some cases, groups bring in a variety of forestry professionals at a very early stage. They bring them in to give presentations or to be part of the audience and ask good questions and provide a reality check on what might work or what might not work.

Lessons Learned

Our forestry cooperative experts were asked if they had any pearls of wisdom they would pass on to others interested in starting a forestry cooperative. Their answers follow.

Gather the Right Group of People

Paul: The time commitment landowners have to devote to this type of project is tremendous. My suggestion would be to make sure you work with a dedicated core group of landowners that are committed to this idea. Active, engaged landowners may be the greatest product that cooperatives produce.

The Massachusetts Woodlands Cooperative has 25 members now and more than 3,000 acres. Of those 25 members, around 15 are very active, each of them bringing unique talent to the group. We have a gentleman who is retired that has done a lot of professional organization and grant writing in his day and has brought that to the table. We have people that run a portable sawmill, a landowner who brings that to the table, we have a professor who teaches design work at a local college who has been very helpful in designing logos and so forth. And so, each landowner really does bring kind of a unique gift and talent to the group. And capitalizing on that, I think, allows the stakeholders to really take ownership of it. Foresters are constantly trying to bring landowners into active forest management on our terms, usually based on growing timber. The co-op model allows people to engage their properties, while helping the greater cause of forestry, on their terms, be it grant writing, graphic design, or wood processing.

Katie: In my opinion, if you have at least three people in that area who want to do something, you've got plenty of interest. You don't need 100; you don't need 200. Sometimes it's better to start small because it's very difficult early on to know what you can promise people. If you have a dozen, that's a real nice number because there are a lot of different people there that can volunteer for different things and cover a lot of bases. As long as you have a handful, you have a place to start because a handful of people have a lot of friends and sit around a lot of kitchen tables and coffee tables and coffee shops and can talk it up plenty. If there's really no interest, if there's only one person in the community that likes this and everyone thinks they're crazy, then I say just wait. Just wait and see if there's something else you can do besides a formal co-op.

I think that one of the biggest keys to success for a co-op project is the leadership. It's a very challenging thing for co-ops to balance leadership roles because a co-op, by nature, is very democratic. But every organization needs someone to spearhead change and to spearhead new ideas to make progress. I think one of the things that I've seen co-ops benefit from a great deal is board training—training people in effective communication and meeting management to help the group stay on task and stay focused on the things that need to get done.

E.G.: Without good local leaders—volunteer steering committee members, board members, and paid staff—a lot of good co-op ideas are likely to fail or have a difficult time getting off the ground. Without mentioning the name of the co-op, one story illustrates this point. The co-op's first coordinator turned out not to be very committed to the job. He didn't do much for about nine months. Then the board decided to hire a replacement. He had the right skills, but, for whatever reason, never really got focused on the project and quit after a few months. Then the board hired a third coordinator. He's been there for over three years and is doing a superb job. The co-op is now operating effectively. So, launching a successful co-op has a whole lot to do with finding the right coordinator or manager and having a board of directors committed to what they are doing.

I wouldn't be discouraged about low attendance at initial meetings. Bringing in a large number of landowner-members can occur at some later stage. It doesn't need to happen in the early stages. I think the time to be discouraged though is if the steering committee goes through a lot of work, develops a basic plan for the organization, does a lot of promotion and advertising, and then very few people show up to a potential member meeting; that would be a time to be concerned. You'd need to either look back

One of the areas which I think led to our demise was the fact that we did not have that one individual, that entrepreneurial individual that would take the leadership of the co-op.

Sustainable Woods Cooperative Member

and see whether or not you did an adequate job of promoting the event, or you may have to conclude that there just isn't enough interest in what you are trying to do.

Keep the Members Informed

Katie: The steering committee and the co-op board need to constantly get feedback from their membership. With co-ops, the annual meetings should be very open and allow for some element of discussion. One co-op I work with does a very good job of having their board meetings very well publicized so that the members are able to attend all of those board meetings and get input to the board continually, not just once a year at the annual meeting. To get people to board meetings the little things count, like having them in the evenings, having them on Saturdays or having them followed-up or started by an education walk in the woods or an informational event so that there's motivation for members to come to those meetings. Co-ops are member organizations, and they rely on member support and member enthusiasm.

Have a Clear Mission

Katie: Many times communities come together around an idea in response to community turmoil or stress. Maybe it's that some major wood industry is failing, or they don't feel that their land is being managed well. But it is important that whatever inspires the co-op is sustaining and is positive and becomes something that the community can really gather around and rally around for the long term. What is our co-op trying to do? What are we trying to address? What are we trying to create change around?

Co-ops sometimes are initiated with a couple of friends, a couple of neighbors or people that have been in the community a long time and have seen things change and say 'you know, we've got to do something about this and I think a co-op might help; I think a landowner group might help us address our forest management concerns, might help us address our marketing constraints.' It's important to get from that informal idea into a structured formalized process in a timely manner. It doesn't have to happen instantly; you don't have to make everything formal at the first meeting. It's important to have an informal environment where all kinds of different ideas are drawn out.

But if you don't formalize a mission statement, it's difficult for people to understand their role and how to participate. When it's formalized, when there's a formal process for nominating people for the board or for the steering committee, when there's a formal process for when and where meetings are held, when all of these things are formalized in a reliable structured way, it's much more predictable and people have a more understandable way of engaging. It's much more transparent and the community can understand the process that's going on.

The most important step in my experience of co-op development is early in the process, doing a really good job with the visioning and the mission statement goals. It's important early in the process to spend a lot of time on that. Too many groups, I think, try and just quickly get something down on paper and make it real broad and general, but it's really an opportunity to articulate what's unique about your group and to be very specific about what your group will do.

Be Sure To Have a Business Plan

Katie: If a co-op is aiming to do some kind of business venture, a business plan becomes very important. Business plans are a critical way of working through all kinds of issues in a structured manner: what are we trying to do, how much do we need to do to afford this, and what are our priorities for staff or for expenditures and whatnot. It helps get everything out on the table and organized.

I think it's also important that business plans be very fluid, and very flexible and that they are constantly revisited. So every 3 months, every 6 months, the board or the steering committee takes out this document, revises it, adds another chapter or updates it in some way, keep notes in the margin, whatever it might be, so that it stays current and stays relevant and doesn't collect dust because if a business plan is done right, it should be a working document.

E.G.: Here are some recipes for disaster:
- If your business plan says that you need $100,000 to launch your co-op and you get $50,000 and you say, 'Oh well, we can muddle through and start with 50.'
- If your business plan says you need to have a competent manager who knows something about the forest industry and you have a nice, friendly manager who doesn't have the background in the industry and you say, 'Oh well, we can make it work with that.'
- If your business plan says you have to identify solid markets where you have signed agreements for products and instead you have a vague sense that maybe this or that company will buy your products and 'It'll work out.'

Make Sure You Choose the Right Business Model

Paul: I would encourage resource managers looking at this to realize that every group of landowners and that every landscape they are trying this in is very different from those in which other cooperatives exist. I would highly recommend taking a look at other business models in the country and take the best from these models and leave the mistakes behind. I have found it very useful to contact people from other cooperatives; everybody has been very open about sharing information. I would encourage you then if you do get one up and going to maintain that openness and share your mistakes and your successes. Lessons can and should be learned from other groups, but ultimately you need to tailor the effort to your particular landscape.

Katie: You can do some things under a co-op that you can or cannot do under an LLC that you can or cannot do as a nonprofit. So some of the debate is about what is this group trying to do, what are our priorities, what are our goals? When you incorporate as a co-op, it limits you in some ways that other structures don't. And one of the innovative approaches that I see increasingly used is to have both a co-op as the business arm of the landowner group and a nonprofit arm that partners with that co-op so that the nonprofit can get funding to hold workshops and educational events. By keeping some of the education and member services a little bit separate from the business operations, they don't compete and bury each other. You're able to divert resources equally.

Is it Worth the Effort?

Paul: As a service forester, what I hoped from the beginning is that the cooperative would help raise the bar in our project area for the quality of work being done so that other landowners could see that it is possible to achieve your objectives, to manage the forest sustainably in an ecologically sensitive way, to add value to forest products, and to keep wood locally and help the local economy. Those are fairly lofty goals, and I would say that in 3 or 4 years, we haven't achieved all of those, but we've seen glimpses of success enough to keep us going.

I'm charged, as I mentioned earlier, with technical assistance and education outreach, and having a group of landowners such as this makes my job much more efficient; being able to deliver the information to one group of landowners, 25 sitting in a room as opposed to running around to 24 different properties, again, makes my job much easier. Likewise, cooperatives provide an economy of scale for technology transfer. For example, most consulting foresters cannot afford to invest the time and money into GIS. Through the co-op, we hope to make technology available to landowner consultants so that they can make the best management decisions for their clients. The same goes for the regulatory portion of my job. Instead of meeting a State minimum under the Forest Cutting Practices Act, we now have a group of landowners achieving FSC Certification Standards, which by far exceed the State minimums.

This has been a very rewarding experience for me professionally in terms of my growth and development, the opportunity to write grants, to work with diverse people on a complex project. It has really been the joy of my professional career so far. Being involved with a project that starts taking a look at some concepts that I only read about in college, landscape level management and so forth, in a predominantly private landowner landscape is very exciting and I'm thrilled to be a part of this.

Katie: Co-ops can really be a way to reach landowners more effectively and more efficiently. They are a group all in one spot, a captive audience, and so you can deliver your message to that group as a whole rather than each landowner individually. And certainly my experience with co-ops shows that the landowners that are members of co-ops tend to be very interested in taking a part—taking a hands-on role in their forest management and so as foresters, that empowers us to do things on the land that maybe otherwise it'd be really tedious, time consuming and economically infeasible to accomplish. That would allow us to do things like the little timber stand improvement projects, small-scale planting projects, some of the invasive species control projects that no one has enough time and money to tackle.

Co-ops can be very challenging for resource managers, for foresters because they are social organizations; it's another kind of a bureaucracy, it's another meeting, another group, and another organization when already we all have so many organizations to deal with. But they have a unique role to play because they are landowner members and they are very local. Resource managers should find ways to work with these groups because they are trying to do something that has the potential to effect change.

E.G.: Working with local forest landowner groups, whether they are co-ops or nonprofit associations, can be frustrating sometimes. But what keeps me coming back is that I really believe there's a need for these kinds of organizations. The vast majority of non-industrial private forest land in the United States is not managed. I firmly believe that getting local landowners together to learn more about their woods, to access services, to work together to improve their forests can be a viable supplement to the other ways in which government and private organizations are trying to assist private landowners. So, that keeps me coming back. The need is there and somehow we have to figure out a good way to meet it.

Learning From the Experiences of Others: Four Forest Landowner Cooperatives Share Their Stories

Pamela Jakes[1]

For a community or group investigating the appropriateness of a cooperative as a means for organizing local landowners to accomplish forest management or marketing objectives, it is useful to hear about the experiences of other communities or cooperatives. For the conference, we put together a series of video case studies, summarizing the stories of four forest landowner cooperatives as told by cooperative members or potential members. A DVD of the video case studies is included with this report. What follows is a brief description of each cooperative, based on the perceptions and insights of the people we interviewed. Also included is an update on progress made by the cooperative since the interviews were conducted in the summer and early fall of 2003.

We've learned a lot from other co-ops. We've learned a lot about not going too fast, not spending too much money, keeping it small, keeping it grassroots, and keeping landowners at the center.

Massachusetts Woodlands Cooperative Member

Massachusetts Woodland Cooperative, LLC

www.masswoodlands.coop

Interviews conducted by Eli Sagor, August 2003

The Story

Since it was incorporated in the summer of 2001, the Massachusetts Woodland Cooperative (MWC) has set the standard for how to bring together private landowners in an organizational structure that promotes economic development while protecting and enhancing the health of forests in the region. In the summer of 1999 a group of forestry professionals from the Massachusetts Department of Conservation and the University of Massachusetts met with local landowners, consulting foresters, loggers, and mill operators to discuss the possibility of forming a forestry landowner cooperative in western Massachusetts. What followed was the formation of a task group to study the feasibility of forming a cooperative. In 2001, after many meetings and a landowner survey, the MWC was established. The Massachusetts laws relating to cooperatives were seen as archaic, so the group formed as a limited liability company that operates as a cooperative. What this means is that they have "cooperative" in their name, that each member of the cooperative has one vote, and that all profits are returned to the cooperative members. A unique step taken by the group was the formation of a nonprofit organization (a 501C3 organization), the Massachusetts Woodlands Institute. This nonprofit organization is completely separate from the cooperative. While the cooperative focuses on business, the institute is free to focus on education, technical assistance, and community economic

---

[1] USDA Forest Service, North Central Research Station, St. Paul, MN, pjakes@fs.fed.us

development. The institute's nonprofit status allows it to apply for grants that may not be available to the cooperative.

Members of the cooperative belong to or participate in other forestry associations—they are members of Tree Farm (www.treefarmsystem.org) and the Massachusetts Forestry Association (www.massforests.org) and have participated in the Forest Stewardship Program (www.fs.fed.us/cooperativeforestry/programs/loa/fsp.shtml), but they find something unique in belonging to a cooperative. The MWC provides many services to its members including forestry services (for example, guiding preparation of forest plans; identifying reliable foresters, loggers, and other operators), ecological services (for example, controlling exotic/invasive species, documenting the history of the land and its uses), marketing services (for example, developing local and regional markets for low-grade material; arranging for wholesale, retail, and discount sales), and educational services (for example, providing publications and training in the use of forestry equipment). Through all these activities, the guiding star of the MWC is sustainable forestry, and its practice and implementation through Forest Stewardship Council (FSC) green certification.

Members see sustainable forestry as analogous to organic farming. Where 15 or 20 years ago organic farmers could recover the extra costs of producing their products through higher prices, now they receive a premium. MWC members are focused on producing value-added, FSC-certified products with the hope that their cooperative will be well positioned to take advantage of thoughtful customers who care about the health of the world's forests.

Members of the MWC are aware of the economic and business elements that are necessary for them to succeed. They are excited about opportunities to come together as a buying group and a selling group, opportunities that are not found in other forest landowner associations. As a buying group, members can achieve economies of scale not available to individual landowners. As a selling group, they are investigating how they can produce a value-added product that is of high quality, is competitive, and in demand. Members are developing a strong marketing plan that focuses on the story behind the product.

The MWC has developed partnerships that are critical to obtaining necessary services. Professors and extension professionals from the University of Massachusetts-Amherst (www.umass.edu) have provided advice and technical assistance related to forest inventory, wood technology and potential products, and green certification. Additional help with green certification has been provided by SmartWood (www.rainforest-alliance.org/programs/forestry/smartwood). Foresters from the Massachusetts Bureau of Forestry (www.mass.gov/dcr/stewardship/forestry) were critical to initiating the effort. The Hilltown Community Development Corporation (www.hilltowncdc.org), New England Forestry Foundation (www.neforestry.org), and

Community Involved in Sustaining Agriculture (CISA) (www.buylocalfood.com) have also provided key assistance. Local sawmills and other businesses have been important partners. In each instance the key was finding an individual in the organization who had a personal interest in the cooperative and who was in a position to bring resources (expertise, equipment, dollars) to the effort.

Members think the future looks bright for the MWC. They feel they have learned much from the experiences of other cooperatives, and they will succeed if they move slowly, not take on a lot or debt, and look for niche products they can produce efficiently and with high quality.

I see the co-op as being a major step in the education of the American people. Everyone around here, we need to work together cooperatively if we're going to see the planet survive. Having a co-op, I think, is one of the strongest ways we can do that.

Massachusetts Woodlands Cooperative Member

The Update

In January 2004, the MWC was awarded a 3-year, $499,253 grant from the U.S. Department of Agriculture. The goal of this grant is to expand niche markets for MWC that focus on Forest Stewardship Council (FSC) green-certified materials and other value-added forest products. Project activities include:

Development of niche markets. Develop and implement MWC niche markets for flooring, timber frame materials, and residual wood products (e.g., bark mulch, firewood, and pallet wood). This will be accomplished by gathering, sorting, and marketing logs according to grade and species and processing selected logs into value-added products.

Green certification. MWC is already green certified under the group certification process provided by the FSC. However, to market the cooperative's value-added products as green certified, MWC will also need to apply for and receive group chain-of-custody certification from FSC. This will require (1) development of a system for monitoring forest materials as they are transformed into value-added products; and (2) establishing a network of value-added producers who are interested in obtaining FSC-certified wood from the cooperative.

Database development. Expand the MWC database so that it will (1) provide detailed information on forest material that is available for harvesting from MWC members; (2) monitor forest materials as they are transformed into value-added products; (3) organize information needed for the cooperative to function as a business (cost of goods purchased, inventory, sales, marketing, etc.), and (4) link the database with the MWC Web site so that MWC members and those who work on their land can have password access to information about the property.

Expansion of membership and land base. MWC currently has 30 members who together manage around 5,000 acres of forest land. MWC will expand its membership base to 125 members with over 20,000 acres of forest land and identify 25 regional artisans, craftspeople, and other woodworkers who will (1) become associate members of MWC, (2) receive Group FSC chain-of-custody certification as a part of their membership, and (3) create value-added products from FSC green-certified material that is harvested from MWC member forests.

Biomass assessment. Assess the market potential for the use of forest-based biomass fuels in southern New England by analyzing supply and cost data for forest-based biomass fuels.

Information dissemination. Compile, organize, and disseminate information about MWC.

The USDA grant has provided MWC with the working capital needed to accomplish the above tasks. With this grant, MWC has hired employees, supported interns from the University of Massachusetts, established and operated an office, provided partial support for FSC Certification Assessment, and financed an initial inventory of value-added products.

Western Upper Peninsula Forest Improvement District
Interviews conducted by Pamela Jakes, September 2003

The Story

The main reason I see for new members coming to WUPFID now is they feel that they can trust our organization to do the right job for them.

Western Upper Peninsula Forest Improvement District Staff Member

In the late 1970s, the State of Michigan was going through a recession. When the legislature started looking for ways to improve the State's economy, they saw Michigan's vast forest lands and the diverse and potentially valuable forest products those lands could provide. They commissioned a Finnish consulting firm to determine what could be done to improve the health of Michigan's forests and to inject new vitality into the State's economy. The firm recommended the establishment of forest improvement districts, modeled after those found in northern Europe. Legislators recognized the concept of forest improvement districts as similar to the old farmers' cooperatives that were so successful in the Upper Great Lakes States. Forest improvement districts would assist small private landowners, who hold more than half of Michigan's forest land, in managing their forest land, producing healthier forests, and generating raw material that would help stimulate forest product industries. In October 1995, The Western Upper Peninsula Forest Improvement District (WUPFID) was organized as a 5-year pilot study.

Although WUPFID referred to itself as a cooperative and is often cited as the first forestry cooperative in the U.S., it lacks many of the standard characteristics of a cooperative—although members make up the board of directors, WUPFID is not actually owned by its members, and there is no profit sharing among members. It operates more as a private consulting firm with a list of clients referred to as members.

Members receive a variety of services—management plans are written, sales planned and administered, and other improvements carried out on the land. Members of WUPFID continue to participate in the organization because they believe that the professionals at WUPFID can be trusted to manage their land according to their objectives. For the many absentee landowners who are members, this trust is critical to their participating in land management activities.

Although WUPFID was meant to be a 5-year pilot project, its success in improving forest management in the region convinced the legislature to extend the project another year. Over those 6 years, WUPFID received approximately $2 million from the State of Michigan. In return, the State has benefited from WUPFID's management of more than 100,000 acres of forest land—land that was not being managed or reaching its productive potential before WUPFID. In addition, WUPFID activities generated jobs and income from the sale of forest products and implementation of management activities. It's been estimated that this $2 million investment has returned more than $100 million to the State.

In the early years, State investment allowed WUPFID to purchase a building and equipment, and employ foresters, technicians, and an office staff. In 2003, WUPFID's paid professional staff was down to two part-time employees—a forester and an office manager. Over the years, all the assets were sold to finance operations. The staff and board are searching for ways to continue to finance the operation. Poor economic times means there will be no additional State funding. Although WUPFID has a membership of 900 and manages more than 150,000 acres, only around 300 members pay the voluntary $20 annual fee. Most of the cooperative's income comes from fees for service, and the staff and the board believe that it would be impossible to raise those fees. Members have other options for obtaining the services they obtain from WUPFID, and the board feels that if rates become too high, members will go elsewhere, eliminating WUPFID's primary source of income.

Despite the funding challenges, members are focused on re-energizing WUPFID through increased publicity. WUPFID staff feel that if they could generate funding to increase visibility, they could recruit more members, thereby generating more income from management of newly enrolled land. Ideas for increasing visibility include holding field trips and creating a demonstration forest that will show potential members the benefits of sustainable forest management. They hope that after 18 years of experience they can continue to provide services that maintain and improve the health of western Upper Peninsula forests.

Here we are, 18 years later, and I think we have finally perfected what we do best. You look around and see healthy forests, and I really believe that we've been a big big part of that. It's really sad to think that we are not going to be here much longer.

Western Upper Peninsula Forest Improvement District Staff Member

The Update

In June 2004, WUPFID ended operations. Given the wood market in the Upper Peninsula and the lack of State funding, the board and staff found it impossible to maintain the office and provide member services. WUPFID records, including management plans and harvesting history, are being stored in the Department of Natural Resources Baraga office. The board of directors will continue to meet annually, preserving the possibility of resurrecting the cooperative if conditions change.

Sustainable Woods Cooperative

http://www.sustainablewoods.com/
Interviews conducted by Mark Rickenbach, June 2003

The Story

I think most of the landowners were looking for the same thing I was looking for. I think we all wanted that camaraderie, wanted to be able to talk over our different management plans with each other and get some feedback. Of course people had been trying different management concepts as well, and we got feedback on the results of that.

Former Sustainable Woods Cooperative Member

The Sustainable Woods Cooperative (SWC) in southwestern Wisconsin was the first group to use a cooperative structure to practice certified forest management to produce and market chain-of-custody wood products. Organized in 1998, the SWC board of directors voted to dissolve the cooperative in 2003. The former members of SWC are committed to sharing their experiences—offering lessons from which others can learn.

When it closed its doors in 2003, SWC had 150 members with more than 120,000 acres in 11 counties in southwestern Wisconsin. There were two type of SWC members—producers and consumers. Producer-members were characterized as landowners who had purchased their property primarily for recreation, but wanted to manage the land to improve forest health. Many members had experienced or seen poor forestry practices on the land and were looking for an alternative management approach. The consumer-members were portrayed as green consumers who liked the idea of purchasing a product that was processed locally and told a story of sustainable management—they wanted to be part of that story.

So what went wrong? The focus of SWC was on manufacturing and education. Manufacturing was producing certified valued-added products, from primarily small diameter or low-quality material from members' high-graded forests that would satisfy consumer demand. SWC members speak of two phases of SWC: the startup phase (1998-2001) and the market development phase (2001-2003). It appears that debt taken on in the startup phase did not allow goals in the market development stage to be realized.

It's well understood that any startup is challenging—the capitalization, cash flow, need to start generating income can be problematic—and the forestry business is particularly challenging. Several members voiced the opinion that SWC moved too quickly into manufacturing—purchasing land, equipment, and hiring staff—in response to members' desire to see something happening. The manufacturing process required great amounts of capital (land, kilns, storage facilities, and equipment), operating funds (salaries, advertising, utilities), and sophisticated expertise to operate. Debt was incurred early on, and the costs of loans from banks, from members, and from a utility company, and the expenses for day-to-day operations eventually sank the cooperative.

Members had several suggestions for other communities considering forest landowner cooperatives. First, start small. Try bringing together a few neighbors who can share time, expertise, and equipment in managing their land. Test some different approaches to collaboration. Try selling a few products, and move on from there. Second, watch out for debt. Be very clear about why you are borrowing the money, and do not give into the temptation to use borrowed funds for other purposes. Third, have a clear idea of the mission of the cooperative. In your rush to create a business, do not lose sight of the importance of member services. By developing a strong record of member service, you build support for the cooperative within the membership. Fourth, start your product development and marketing early. One SWC member said that the attitude was, "if we build the stuff people will buy it." However, when SWC products were available, members found that there were not enough consumers to generate the income necessary to keep the cooperative operating. They had not developed a market for that product or had not analyzed the market to ensure they were producing something for which there was a niche. Finally, tap into those networks that exist to support cooperatives. Groups like the Richland County Economic Development Commission, Cooperative Development Services (http://www.cdsus.coop/), University of Wisconsin Center for Cooperatives (http://www.wisc.edu/uwcc/), and Community Forestry Resource Center (http://www.forestrycenter.org/) all provided valuable services to SWC.

I think the advantage of a co-op versus other organizations is the fact that you are really hands on. I mean, you go to a cooperative meeting and its members are talking about very specific concerns that the co-op has and the members have, and they are all local neighbors... I was needing information on forestry that applies to me and I felt the co-op helped me in that way.

Former Sustainable Woods Cooperative Member

The Update

The Sustainable Woods Cooperative is gone, but there are a group of landowners who continue to meet and share ideas. They are committed to improving the quality of their forests and the landscape—that commitment remains even if the cooperative does not.

Blue Ridge Forest Cooperative

http://nextgenwoods.com/blue_ridge_forest_landowner_coop.htm
Interviews conducted by Eli Sagor, August 2003

The Story

In the Blue Ridge Mountains of Virginia, local landowners are investigating the possibility for encouraging sustainable forest management through a forest landowner cooperative. Many local landowners have had bad experiences with loggers or other woodsworkers, and they are looking for ways to take back control of their forests. They want a management approach for timber and nontimber forest products (ginseng, medicinal plants, recreation) that maintains or improves ecological health while generating income. What these neighbors envision is a vertically integrated organization, member governed, that is certified to do sustainable forest management, harvesting and hauling, and processing, while educating members and the community about options for keeping the three legs of the sustainability stool—forest sustainability, economic sustainability, and social sustainability—in balance.

This infant organization has received advice and support from many quarters. Staff members at the Community Forestry Resource Center (http://www.forestrycenter.org), Appalachian Forest Resource Center (http://www.appalachianforest.org/), and Virginia Department of Forestry (http://www.dof.virginia.gov) have been a great source of information. But the researchers of this idea have found the existing forest landowner cooperatives in Massachusetts, Wisconsin, and elsewhere—others who have been through the process the Virginia group is just beginning—to be their most important partners.

Many questions remain to be answered—What organizational structure will be adopted (it's not clear that this will be a cooperative, as opposed to a limited liability partnership or some other organization)? How large should the membership be? How do they raise capital? But many people feel that the cooperative is off to a good start with a processor already on board and a Forest Stewardship Council (FSC) certified forester interested in participating (www.fsc.org/en). Locals are optimistic about the potential for a cooperative in the Blue Ridge Mountains and what it could mean for their community. They look forward to the interaction people will be having with each other, and the sharing of members' talents, skills, and resources in the sustainable management of their forest land.

The Update

In the past year the Blue Ridge Mountain group has organized as a cooperative under Virginia statutes—the Blue Ridge Forest Cooperative, Inc.

Lewis County, Washington

Interviews conducted by Charlie Blinn, August 2003

The Story

For our last case study we go to southwestern Washington. The Family Forest Foundation (FFF) (http://www.familyforestfoundation.org/) is leading an effort to explore the feasibility of developing a forest landowner cooperative to market trees from non-industrial private forests. Foundation members received a grant from the U.S. Department of Agriculture to conduct a feasibility study in Lewis County. They want to know if landowner interest in a cooperative is sufficient to proceed, if there are enough resources (timber, technical, and human resources), and if markets exist for potential products that might be produced by a cooperative.

Folks in other cooperatives have been very free and open about sharing information—hearing who's made what mistakes and who's had what successes has just been an enormous help. It's going to keep us, hopefully, from making the same mistakes, and allow us to build on the hard knocks others have already gone through.

Potential Blue Ridge Forest Cooperative Member

People who are interested in this cooperative aren't the cut out and get out kind of people, you know. They're someone who's interested in the long-term health of the resource—managing it sustainably and wanting it to endure and be lasting.

Potential Blue Ridge Forest Cooperative Member

Forest landowners in Lewis County already participate in a number of forestry programs, but while these programs offer a diverse assortment of educational programs, they don't function as a business. A cooperative would bring forest landowners together to manage their tree farms collectively as an efficient business and to pool their resources so that they have leverage in the market. Maintaining, improving, and developing markets is the primary reason given for initiating a forest landowner cooperative in Lewis County. In this region, small forest landowners tend to grow larger trees than their industrial neighbors. At this time there are few processors for medium to large diameter trees, hence it's a buyers' market. Marketing, having access to markets, being able to label your products as certified and/or locally produced, and bringing together landowners to more effectively communicate with each other and with policymakers were identified as the most important reasons for starting a cooperative.

Organizers and potential members have learned much from visiting other cooperatives. They see a need for a cooperative clearinghouse where the lessons of different cooperatives can be gathered and shared with other interested parties. One lesson the Lewis County group learned from their visits is to avoid becoming grant dependent. However, they see a significant role for grants in the startup phases of a cooperative. They also know they need to focus on developing a realistic business plan that includes a significant marketing effort in advance of producing a product. They want to create a recognizable brand and educate potential consumers so they can differentiate between a wood product processed locally from wood produced on a local family forest and a product produced elsewhere on some other type of forest.

In addition to these challenges, the Lewis County group will need to overcome the fiercely independent nature of many southwestern Washington landowners. A cooperative is about bringing people together to manage land and run a business cooperatively so overcoming the desire to "do it my way" will be a challenge for building membership and running the cooperative. They also see a need to develop positive, constructive partnerships with local forestry businesses. Professional consulting foresters, in particular, may see a cooperative as a threat, so the cooperative will need to find ways to include these potential partners in the early planning and development stages.

The Lewis County group has identified roles for a number of potential partners—foresters, bankers, lawyers, biologists, other "–ologists." They recognize that forestry is a very complex business and that they will need to draw on the expertise of a diverse group of professionals to make the cooperative work.

For now, the landowners of Lewis County see the year 2004 as being an intensive planning period, and they anticipate having a sound business plan and being in a position to hire a project manager by the end of 2004. Depending on the findings from the feasibility study, they hope to be operating as a cooperative in 2005.

I think that cooperatives would be essential in the long-term survivorship of the family forest. If we don't work and try to establish cooperatives—that, I think, would be a negative in the future of private forest lands.

Lewis County, Washington, Potential Cooperative Member

The Update

The Family Forest Foundation recently completed a feasibility study for a small forest landowner cooperative in southwestern Washington State. The final report for the feasibility study can be found on the Web at: www.familyforestfoundation.org. The results of the feasibility study indicated significant interest among landowners in formally organizing to address a number of forest management needs. Landowners expressed interest in the following services provided by a cooperative: reliable forest management information, estate planning, assistance with complex State and Federal regulations, and forest management planning. The feasibility study identified a number of unique marketing opportunities for logs and value-added forest products; however, organizing to market these products is a complicated prospect and landowners did not express discontent with the current process of marketing and selling logs.

The Family Forest Foundation concluded that before any efforts are made to improve the marketing of forest products from small forest lands, landowners must be organized around a central common principle. Landowners in southwestern Washington identified as their greatest need an approach for minimizing the burden of State and Federal regulations. In response to this need, the foundation is first working to organize landowners around a federally recognized Habitat Conservation Plan (HCP) (http:// endangered.fws.gov/hcp/HCP_Incidental_Take.pdf). The HCP protects a landowner against changes in State and Federal forest management laws if his/her management plan and its implementation reflect state-of-the-art knowledge and regulations at the time it was prepared and carried out. The HCP will also assist landowners with developing a long-term forest management plan. Through the HCP, landowners will inventory their forests and this inventory will provide information for future efforts to find better market opportunities for their logs.